THE **COMPLETE IDIOT'S GUIDE** TO

Reading Body Language

by Susan Constantine

ALPHA

A member of Penguin Group (USA) Inc.

With all my love I dedicate this book to my beautiful daughters Madison and McKenzie. You both are my reason to take a breath each day. I love you, Mom

ALPHA BOOKS

Published by Penguin Group (USA) Inc.

Penguin Group (USA) Inc., 375 Hudson Street, New York, New York 10014, USA • Penguin Group (Canada), 90 Eglinton Avenue East, Suite 700, Toronto, Ontario M4P 2Y3, Canada (a division of Pearson Penguin Canada Inc.) • Penguin Books Ltd., 80 Strand, London WC2R 0RL, England • Penguin Ireland, 25 St. Stephen's Green, Dublin 2, Ireland (a division of Penguin Books Ltd.) • Penguin Group (Australia), 250 Camberwell Road, Camberwell, Victoria 3124, Australia (a division of Pearson Australia Group Pty. Ltd.) • Penguin Books India Pvt. Ltd., 11 Community Centre, Panchsheel Park, New Delhi—110 017, India • Penguin Group (NZ), 67 Apollo Drive, Rosedale, North Shore, Auckland 1311, New Zealand (a division of Pearson New Zealand Ltd.) • Penguin Books (South Africa) (Pty.) Ltd., 24 Sturdee Avenue, Rosebank, Johannesburg 2196, South Africa • Penguin Books Ltd., Registered Offices: 80 Strand, London WC2R 0RL, England

Copyright © 2013 by Alpha Books

International Standard Book Number: 978-1-61564-248-9
Library of Congress Catalog Card Number: 2012951747

15   14   13   8   7   6   5   4   3   2   1

Interpretation of the printing code: The rightmost number of the first series of numbers is the year of the book's printing; the rightmost number of the second series of numbers is the number of the book's printing. For example, a printing code of 13-1 shows that the first printing occurred in 2013.

Printed in the United States of America

Note: This publication contains the opinions and ideas of its author. It is intended to provide helpful and informative material on the subject matter covered. It is sold with the understanding that the author and publisher are not engaged in rendering professional services in the book. If the reader requires personal assistance or advice, a competent professional should be consulted.

The author and publisher specifically disclaim any responsibility for any liability, loss, or risk, personal or otherwise, which is incurred as a consequence, directly or indirectly, of the use and application of any of the contents of this book.

Most Alpha books are available at special quantity discounts for bulk purchases for sales promotions, premiums, fundraising, or educational use. Special books, or book excerpts, can also be created to fit specific needs. For details, write: Special Markets, Alpha Books, 375 Hudson Street, New York, NY 10014.

Publisher: *Mike Sanders*

Executive Managing Editor: *Billy Fields*

Senior Acquisitions Editor: *Tom Stevens*

Development Editor: *Susan Zingraf*

Senior Production Editor: *Kayla Dugger*

Copy Editor: *Tricia Liebig*

Cover Designer: *William Thomas*

Book Designers: *William Thomas, Rebecca Batchelor*

Indexer: *Johnna VanHoose Dinse*

Layout: *Brian Massey*

Proofreader: *Jeanne Clark*

Contents

Appendixes

Introduction

This is where it all began over a decade ago. I bought my first book on how to read body language. As a jury consultant, I wanted to know how to read jurors better.

Armed with my new knowledge, I watched the prospective jurors as they entered the courtroom, single file, and filled the gallery—pierced tattoo guy, the CEO in his pressed navy-blue suit, the football coach, the homemaker, the cash-strapped single mother, the retiree, the grandmother, the woman who looked like she'd had a really tough life, the small business owner, the college student, the military retiree ... the list goes on.

We had to pick 12, but which ones? I listened carefully as each juror gave a five-minute rundown of their life and worldview. I paid attention and made notes on their tone, voice inflection, punctuation, and how well they articulated their words.

Their facial expressions were a newly opened book to me as the judge styled the case and read the charge—murder in the first degree! I could actually *see* their feelings—some surprised, others saddened; one had a smirk on her face, another scratched his neck.

I felt like Sherlock Holmes with his magnifying glass, examining every facial tic, and the way each prospective juror held his or her hands, arms, and legs—all clues to what they might be thinking and feeling.

Applying what I'd learned, I made my juror selections, marveling at how much my new knowledge of body language helped the pieces fall into place—revelations I can't wait to share with you.

As your body language mentor, I will guide you through as we embark on this journey together in the amazing study of human communication. Many of the scenarios are true experiences drawn from my mediation practice, my time in the courtroom, my own family, and stories I have heard from clients who have attended my training seminars.

This is not the quick fix or seven-day plan that promises your life will forever be changed if you follow these steps and techniques. Rather this book is based on the realities of everyday life, remaining authentic and true and based on solid research, not merely subjective opinion.

How This Book Is Organized

Part 1, Silent Messages, begins with a body language boot camp. You'll learn the truths and myths about reading body language in a fun, easy-to-read format that will keep you engaged. You'll learn how to build and maintain rapport with anyone and have them eating out of your hands. You'll learn why you missed the clues and our natural ability to retain, capture, and store information in our brains. You'll learn how to read the muscles in other people's faces that are dead giveaways to know how they are feeling, a powerful negotiation skill in every walk of life. You'll discover how your first impression sends a strong message about your character, abilities, and trustworthiness. What you wear can expose your age, income, and secrets you might not even know about yourself. We'll share the do's and don'ts when applying for a job interview or going on a date, as well as the meaning behind different handshakes.

Part 2, Body Talk, begins to dig a bit deeper into how you communicate and process information. You'll learn how to read another's eye movements through seeing, hearing, and feeling. Along the way, you'll do a few exercises to see how well you're learning the information. You'll learn the meanings behind cultural gestures, as well as norms of what to do and not do when traveling around the world or simply encountering people of other cultures in your neighborhood. And when you travel back to the United States, you'll learn how to use hand and arm gestures to convey your message to others to lead, motivate, inspire, and persuade them in business negotiations, sales, and everyday relationships. Next, look down at your feet because you'll learn whether you're ready to take a hike or you're taking life one step at a time.

Part 3, Deception Detection, is all about reading deception, motives, and intent. You'll learn why kids lie, from small white lies to big fat whoppers, and when you should be concerned and when not to worry. This part gets to the heart of what everyone is curious about. How can I tell if I'm being duped, cheated on, or getting the run around? You'll learn how to read voice, words, and phrases. You'll learn how to decipher excuses people give you and what they are really revealing. After reading this part, you'll no longer be looking through rose-colored glasses; it will all be crystal clear.

Part 4, Strictly Business, teaches you to how to successfully navigate a job interview from start to finish to land you that dream job you're after. You'll also learn how to handle negotiations and read negotiation tactics, buy signs, and signs of resistance. You'll learn how effective speakers move about the room and use space as a powerful tool to anchor a message. You'll learn when the deal is heading south, and how to change your course to seal the deal. Then we move on to relationships—how to read love signals, as well as red flags that it's over.

Extras

Additional information is found in sidebars within each chapter. Here's what you'll find:

WORKIN' IT

Helpful body language tips and techniques.

BODY BLOCK

Common mistakes and cautions regarding the use of certain body language skills.

SAY WHAT?

Quotes and definitions pertaining to the subject matter.

YA DON'T SAY

Interesting asides and water-cooler–worthy insights.

Acknowledgments

A special thanks to my dynamic duo, Brad and Darlyn Kuhn of Brad Kuhn & Associates in Orlando, Florida. Your talents and creative writing and editing make my words jump off the page to deliver the true essence of my message to my readers.

I'm so grateful to Jeff Hegarty Photography for Jeff's exceptional artistic creative abilities in capturing all the images and photos in this book. Your work makes the text come alive with visuals throughout the book.

Thanks to Jill Hegarty, owner of Twist Hair Studio in Orlando, Florida, for providing the photography studio and locations for the photo shoots, as well as hair and make-up for the models and actors. Thanks to personal hairdresser Jill Hegarty and stylists Jax St. Ledger, Megan Gregory, Lindsey Dixon, Audrey Weech, and Julian Montalvo for making us all look fabulous!

Likewise, gratitude is due to Maile Professional Image, Modeling & Acting School in Winter Park, Florida, and to Debbie Wisner, school owner, for providing the majority of the professional actors and models for the book. Thanks, Deb!

A special thanks to all my actors and models. Your dedication and time devoted to the project were overwhelming and deeply appreciated.

Dr. David Matsumoto and daughter Sayaka Matsumoto—thank you both for your training materials in reading facial expressions and intercultural communications. I am proud to be an affiliate trainer for your company, Humintell.

Thank you, Dr. James Pennebaker, for your contribution by providing your research and graph for reading the words people say, as author of *The Secret Life of Pronouns*.

Warm thanks to literary agent Marilyn Allen, who contacted me when searching for the perfect writer for *The Complete Idiot's Guide to Reading Body Language*. You're a beautiful soul and an inspiration. Thank you so much for the wonderful opportunity and for making this all happen. And thank you, Tom Stevens, senior acquisitions editor at Alpha Books, for being a kind mentor, guiding me along the whole way.

To Jim Duke, Retired Lieutenant, New Jersey State Police, my best friend and colleague. Jim is my go-to person when I need a fresh set of eyes, support, and guidance as well as the technical writer for this book. I love you, Jim!

I appreciate my parents, Carol and John Kane, for always being there unconditionally. Love you both!

Most of all, to the loves of my life, my children. Thank you, my two beautiful daughters, Madison and McKenzie Faller, for supporting Mom all the way and putting up with my time spent plugging away on the computer. You are who I live for and my reason to take a breath each morning. My message each day to my girls is: "There is nothing you could ever say or do that would make me stop loving you. Thank you for giving my life meaning and purpose. Love you, Mommy."

Special Thanks to the Technical Reviewer

The Complete Idiot's Guide to Reading Body Language was reviewed by an expert who double-checked the accuracy of what you'll learn here, to help us ensure that this book gives you everything you need to know about body language. Special thanks are extended to Jim Duke.

Trademarks

All terms mentioned in this book that are known to be or are suspected of being trademarks or service marks have been appropriately capitalized. Alpha Books and Penguin Group (USA) Inc. cannot attest to the accuracy of this information. Use of a term in this book should not be regarded as affecting the validity of any trademark or service mark.

Silent Messages

We've all heard the term "body language," but what does that actually mean? Part 1 explores body language myths and truths, with warnings against common assumptions, and gives you basic training in rapport building and other useful techniques.

First impressions are lasting, and you'll discover how body language cues such as your handshake, your walk, and your eye contact can make or break the impression you make. Likewise, fascinating facts about appearance are explored, and you'll find out that the colors you wear can affect how trustworthy you appear.

Finally, the facial expressions that reveal emotions are explored. You'll learn to determine learning styles, and how to put that knowledge to use reading communication styles through body language.

Body Language Basics

In This Chapter

- What reading body language is and what it isn't
- How to avoid assumptions and blindness
- What the five-step process is to reading people

Body language experts are not psychics, and they can't read minds. No one but Pinocchio has a built-in lie detector, and Pinocchio is a fictional character.

In the world of reading body language, we have just two rules:

1. There is no one definitive way to tell if someone is lying.

2. If anyone says there is, they're lying.

Everything else, as with body language itself, is subject to interpretation. Body linguistics is not judging or predicting. It is the interpretation of thoughts and feelings externalized through a combination of cues—gestures, facial expressions, spoken words, and tone of voice. Part art and part science, reading body language is a combination of subjective and objective analyses based on grounded research.

In this chapter, you learn basic concepts that are fundamental in building a foundation for reading body language, including understanding assumptions, inherent blindness, and the process of connecting with other people.

No Smoking Gun

There is no one bodily gesture that has a single definitive meaning, so that leaves a lot of room for interpretation. As it turns out, with the possible exception of professional poker players, most people are notoriously bad at reading each other.

Research reveals that the average person's ability to read body language is no more accurate than flipping a coin—and that includes county judges, police officers, and clinical psychologists. Federal judges and secret service professionals, however, do a better job at it, but they have lots of experience. With proper training, a person's accuracy rate in reading body language can increase to 76 percent or higher.

YA DON'T SAY

There is no one gesture that is a dead giveaway when it comes to reading someone.

Myths and Truths

Have you ever judged someone unfairly? Upon meeting someone, did you sum them up in a microsecond, only to discover later that you were way off base? It happens to the best of us.

BODY BLOCK

Having the ability to read people accurately is a powerful tool. But with great power comes great responsibility. Keep the skills you learn in perspective, and use them responsibly.

Making the wrong assessment about someone can be embarrassing and frustrating, so let's clarify some myths and truths about reading body language to help you get started on the right foot.

Myths about body language include:

- Body language gestures have specific meanings.
- Reading body language is a natural ability.

- Averted or shifty eyes are signs of lying.
- Scratching the nose is a sign of lying.
- Liars make less eye contact.

Truths about body language include:

- Most body language gestures have multiple meanings.
- Reading body language is a learned skill.
- "Locking" eyes is a signal of convincing, rather than conveying.
- Scratching the face is a sign of anxiety.
- Liars often make more eye contact, not less.

YA DON'T SAY

The average person has about a 50 percent accuracy rate when reading others. Often, people make false assumptions about others without gathering all the relevant information before coming to a conclusion.

Don't Make Assumptions

Some people are simply in the wrong place at the wrong time. For example, a witness describes a 6'2" white male with blond hair, approximately 200 pounds, last seen leaving a home invasion in a blue car.

Minutes later, a blue car pulls up to a convenience store one block away. A man hops out to pump gas. He has blond hair and matches the description. The victim positively identifies him as the perpetrator. "That's the guy; I'm sure of it!" she says.

Police question the man but let him go. Despite the physical similarities, the victim had pegged the wrong man.

This is an example of someone jumping to a conclusion without first having all the necessary information and making an assumption—and the assumption is wrong.

> **WORKIN' IT**
>
> When reading body language, you are a silent observer, not a tattle-tale, so keep it in perspective. Avoid making false assumptions or judgments. Reading people is not judging someone's character; rather it is the careful observation of behaviors in others. Something that seems obvious to you may not be what it seems. Gather all the information before making your analysis.

Getting an Accurate Read

Have you ever watched a movie you loved, over and over again, and each time you watched it, you picked up something new?

Reading body language is like that. To read people more accurately, you should, ideally, observe them repeatedly over time. It is important to know what to look for so you'll be able to pick up more clues in less time.

> **BODY BLOCK**
>
> There is no body language "quick fix." Some people believe that you can just look at someone and in seconds have the person all figured out; that's not true. Body language interpretation is a study of contrasts and inconsistencies. Before you detect deception, you need to establish a baseline of "normal" behaviors for comparison.

Think about what happens when you visit a doctor. You or a nurse writes down your symptoms. The doctor reviews your chart, has a brief chat with you, and examines you physically before delivering a diagnosis. It's a step-by-step process.

Reading people is very much the same. You consider the context (why you're here), the verbal content (tell me what's wrong), and non-verbal cues (examination). Then you analyze the data to form your opinion (diagnosis).

Here's a little self-test. Look at the following photo for a few minutes. What information can you gather from it? What kind of work do you think the man in the picture does? What does he sell? What kind of product does he promote? What can you gather about his organizational skills? Look at his facial expressions. Is he a nice guy, or is he rigid? What do think his position is? Is he a manager, a CEO? What could the hand signify? Why are there trucks on the wall?

Find the clues.

You can check your answers in Appendix B.

How Clues Are Missed

Have you ever realized in hindsight something that totally was obvious, yet you completely missed it at the time? There's a reason we sometimes miss the obvious; it's called *inattentive blindness*. It's the same phenomenon that causes a texting driver to sit through an entire green light.

SAY WHAT?

Inattentive blindness is the failure to fully notice an unexpected object because one's attention is focused on another object or event.

It can be embarrassing—like that time you spaced out when the boss was talking to you because you were making weekend plans in your head. Inattentive blindness can also be dangerous—like the woman who didn't see the stranger approaching in a dark parking lot because she was busy digging in her purse for her car keys.

Inattentive blindness can be dangerous.

It is impossible to be fully attentive to two things at once. That's one reason it can be so hard to read someone, if you are also talking to them or trying to listen to what they are saying. The best way to study body language is as a passive observer, such as just watching someone from across the room. This allows you to simply observe from a distance and not be thinking about anything else.

It's hard to be attentive to what someone's saying when you are also trying to focus on something else, such as watching TV.

Basic Training: Five Steps to Reading People

If you want to be able to accurately read someone, you need to make the person feel comfortable with you first. When someone is comfortable with you, they will be more relaxed and open. The following step-by-step process gives you a basic framework for learning how to create these circumstances that will give you the ability to more accurately read what someone is really saying.

Step 1—Building Rapport

Ask any investigator how they extract information from a suspect. What they will tell you is that it all begins with rapport building. When you meet someone, never come right out and get to the point. If you do, you will kill the rapport-building stage. When you jump right in, it becomes your agenda, not theirs. When a skilled investigator interviews a suspect, they never begin with saying "You're a liar; I know you did it!" That tactic is only seen in the movies, and it rarely works.

For better results, slow things down. Talk about neutral topics—the bad coffee in the cafeteria, sports, fashion, the weather. Show interest in them as a person, not just a prospect or perpetrator. Casually observe the person's attire. A compliment on a watch, lapel pin, piece of jewelry, or piece of fashionable clothing often helps ease the initial anxiety.

An easy and quick way to establish rapport is to address a person by their name. This demonstrates that you are interested in the person and care about what they have to say. But use the name sparingly, as overusage may be viewed as disingenuous and phony.

Rapport building is the essence of a positive outcome. It's not only used in law enforcement to catch the bad guys, but in every aspect of human communication, whether it's sales prospecting, coaching, training, management, or dating.

Some of the best rapport builders are hair stylists. Next time you visit your stylist, watch the interaction between the hairdressers and their clients. Hair stylists are masters of rapport. From the minute they run their fingers through a client's hair, they're exchanging life histories.

Part beautician, part psychotherapist, a hair stylist knows whom everyone is dating, what so-and-so are doing this weekend, what movies they've seen, who's in trouble with the IRS, and the names and ages of everyone's kids.

People open up to, and do business with, people they like and trust. It all starts with building a good rapport. You know it works because not many people choose to do business with people they dislike.

Hair stylists are masters of rapport.

YA DON'T SAY

Marie Laveau, the famous New Orleans voodoo queen, was a hair dresser by trade. Scholars who have studied her alleged voodoo powers suggest that perhaps her greatest and only power was nothing more than an extraordinary gift for extracting information from her clients and using that information to her advantage.

Step 2—Mirroring

A natural *mirroring* of body language occurs when two people connect on a cellular level. When there's a connection, the two synchronize their body language like a choreographed dance. It is unexplained, yet it is seen throughout nature.

 SAY WHAT?

Mirroring is the conscious reflection of the sameness of another.

Penguins follow in a single-file line; birds fly in patterns; and fish swim in unison. Couples who like each other tend to match the body language of their partner. For example, when one leans forward to reach for a glass, the other, without thinking, will do the same thing. Some couples even unconsciously synchronize what they wear. When building rapport, you should always mirror some aspect of the other's behavior.

 WORKIN' IT

Try this marker of rapport: when you think you're in sync with someone, shift position, and watch for him or her to shift as well. If they do not shift or move when you do, you're not in sync. Repeat until your motions align.

Matching mannerisms, or mirroring, is a technique for building rapport.

The five ways to mirror someone are …

- Adopting (loosely) the mannerisms of the person you're try-ing to mirror.

- Synchronizing your breathing with theirs.

- Matching voice tone and inflection.

- Empathizing—meeting energy with energy and concern with concern.

- Echoing key words and speaking at a common level.

Step 3—Norming

Norming is a process of assessing another's normal behavior patterns during rapport building.

 SAY WHAT?

Norming means establishing the normal behavioral patterns of another in a neutral, nonconfrontational environment.

Norming is the process of observing behaviors during rapport build-ing. As you talk about those neutral topics, mentally take note of the interviewee's normal speech and voice patterns, gestures, and language.

For example, if, in the person's norm, you see any signs of facial tics, speech errors, or anxiousness, these could be quirks in their normal behavior and should not be interpreted out of context as anything unusual.

Your goal is to get the individual as close to normal behavior patterns as possible. You won't know a person's absolute norm unless you have an intimate personal relationship with that person.

Step 4—Baselining

Typical behaviors observed during the norming stage become the "baseline" from which we compare and contrast behavior patterns.

Although it is possible to establish a good baseline, even in a tense situation, establishing rapport is especially important to alleviate anxiety that might otherwise alter normal behaviors.

> **BODY BLOCK**
>
> Easy does it! If you come forth in attack mode, it will be almost impossible to find a baseline.

Immigration officers have to be especially skilled at speed-reading complete strangers and putting them at ease, because they have five minutes or less to determine whether or not to allow them to enter the country.

Actual questions from an immigration screening are likely to start with nonthreatening inquiries, such as, "Did you find a good parking spot?" or "Boy, it looks like you're ready for a great family vacation, with all those bags."

During the norming period, officers establish a baseline by reading facial expressions, body language, voice, and words, before moving on to more pointed questions, such as, "What is the purpose of your visit?" and "What preparations have you made prior to coming to the United States?"

Step 5—Comparing and Contrasting Behaviors

Once you've established a baseline, you can move into more direct questioning. As the questions become more pointed, look for changes in the subject's behavior. These changes are usually subtle—twitches, twinges, and muscle contractions. These are signs of *leakage* or contrasting behaviors that might indicate deception, anxiety, or concern.

> **SAY WHAT?**
>
> **Leakage** is nonverbal gestures betraying concealed emotions. For example, suppressed tears and sadness may leak out through self-pacifying gestures like rubbing a leg, stroking hair, or rubbing thumbs together.

Only after comparing and contrasting behaviors to the baseline, and considering all of the factors that could contribute to those variances, should you even begin to draw conclusions.

Field Exercise: A Client Meeting

There are several examples throughout this book showing you how you can directly apply what you are learning in your day-to-day life. The following exercise illustrates how to hone in on a client's needs and expectations using the concepts you learned in this chapter.

In some ways people are pretty predictable. We all want to be heard. We want to be understood. And we like to do business with people who "get" us. This is why rapport building is a crucial step in doing business, or anything in life for that matter.

When a client or potential client wants to meet, start the rapport-building process off right by asking him where he'd like to meet. He will choose a location that is most comfortable for him, be it his favorite coffee shop, his favorite restaurant, or his office.

When you arrive, shake hands firmly, look the client in the eye, smile, and offer a warm greeting. Find something positive to say. Exude energy. People like to be around people who are positive and confident. Take a few minutes to get to know your client. Don't be too eager to dive right into the business at hand.

Watch your client closely during those first few minutes. Remember, in addition to building rapport, you are norming—establishing a baseline against which you'll be comparing behaviors during the more direct business discussion later.

Take special note of any quirks, tics, or nervous habits, so that you won't be as likely to misread them later.

As you build rapport, look for signs of mirroring as well. If your client's movements are in synch with yours, that's a sign that you have established a connection and it is time to move on to the business at hand.

Once you enter the formal discussion phase, be on the lookout for changes in gestures and facial expressions—such changes are signs of emotional leakage. They could indicate excitement, or agitation. You'll learn in subsequent chapters how to tell the difference.

The Least You Need to Know

- Accurately reading body language requires training and practice.
- Reading body language is not judging others or making assumptions.
- The average person is not very good at reading others.
- There are five basic steps for reading people: building rapport, mirroring, norming, baselining, and comparing and contrasting behaviors.

First Impressions

In This Chapter

- How first impressions are the most lasting
- Which quick fixes can improve first impressions
- How handshakes can make or break you

You know first impressions are important. That's one of the reasons you're reading this book. But do you know how quickly and permanently people form opinions about you before you even speak a single word?

One minute. That's how long it takes people to size you up upon first meeting you. If that seems unfair, consider that you're doing the same to them.

What your body says in that first minute—your facial expressions, your voice, your grooming, and the way you dress—will be the basis on which people form lasting impressions of your character, personality, income, and education.

In this chapter, you learn the things you do with your body that communicate volumes about yourself and how to fix your body movements and actions to make good first impressions.

Snap Judgments

Using a scenario of attending a networking meeting, let's see how body language says more than words could ever say.

It's half past seven on a bright Monday morning. You're fresh, pressed, and dressed your best as you pull into the parking lot for the monthly Chamber of Commerce networking breakfast. Fluff the hair, check. Breath mint, check. Business cards, check. Elevator speech, check. Elevator image, ch … wait, my what? Read on.

In a couple of minutes you're going to walk into a building and try to convince a bunch of people you've never met to do business with you. You want to impress them as a confident, competent, and personable business person.

You've got your elevator speech—that Toastmasters summary of who you are, what you do, and why they should do business with you, short enough to deliver between floors on an elevator (thus the name). It should roll off your tongue with passion, humility, and authenticity. That's a good start.

But it's your elevator image—that all-important combination of dress, facial expressions, grooming, gestures, and tone of voice—that will leave the true lasting impression.

YA DON'T SAY

The words you speak account for only a small fraction of what you communicate—only 7 percent, in fact. Studies show people send and receive up to 4,000 messages an hour, with internal responses expressed externally through facial muscles, gestures, body movements, and tone of voice. Fifty-five percent of the messages you send to others are conveyed through body language; 38 percent through the tone, pace, rhythm, and inflection of your voice.

Your first impression is going to stick in the minds of others and it rarely changes. Psychologists say this is a primal instinct—like fight or flight—originating in the amygdala, one of the oldest parts of the brain.

The good news is that you're in control of how you present yourself.

People make snap judgments about you every day.

Ten Quick Fixes for Great First Impressions

In a business setting, a new suit is sharp, and the shine on those shoes gets you extra points. But your success will ultimately depend on a combination of the image you convey and how well you read the messages others are sending you.

The following quick fixes will help get you started right away in understanding body language, both your own and what you observe of others. We will cover the various body parts in further detail in Part 2.

Quick Fix #1—Personal Assessment

First of all, to be able to create a good first impression on others, you have to get real with yourself. Ask yourself:

- Am I as successful as I want to be?

- When was the last time someone said I impressed them?

- When was the last time someone said they remembered meeting me before?

Now take the following Personal Assessment Quiz to get a true picture of yourself, which will help you make the necessary adjustments.

1. What is the appropriate amount of eye contact in a face-to-face encounter?

    A. 50–70 percent

    B. 70–80 percent

    C. 80–100 percent

2. When making eye contact with your customer, where do you focus your eyes?

    A. From the tip of the nose to the outer corners of the eyes

    B. From the tip of the nose to the mouth

    C. Glance at different places around the face

    D. Don't have a clue

3. Which best describes your handshaking style?

    A. Hand on top pressing down toward the ground

    B. Grasping with both hands, one on either side

    C. I don't shake hands unless I have to

    D. None of the above

4. How do you prefer to make a sales pitch?

    A. Tell the customer about our company and services; when I'm finished I ask them questions

    B. Ask the customer a series of questions to understand their needs and budget

    C. Build rapport and trust first; then ask the customer to tell me about his or her business

5. When listening to a customer's complaint, I ...

    A. Play it cool, don't sweat the small stuff, and keep my face expressionless

    B. Lean slightly forward; tilt my head occasionally; and nod, signaling I understand

    C. Lean back, taking it all in, and sometimes cross my arms

6. What color do you wear to build trust?

    A. Green

    B. Blue

    C. White

    D. Whatever color I feel like wearing that day

7. Which best describes the way you would present a proposal to a customer face-to-face?

    A. Hand the customer the proposal, with a pen to sign it

    B. Place the proposal in an envelope, and slide it to the customer to open

    C. Place the proposal in the center of the table, and let the customer reach for it

8. If you are a man, when meeting a prospect, what would you wear?

    A. A power suit

    B. Dress pants, sport coat, buttoned shirt, and tie

    C. Khaki pants and a polo shirt

    D. None of the above

If you are a woman, what would you wear to meet a male business prospect?

A. Pantsuit with a blouse

B. Dress with a jacket

C. Skirt suit and camisole

D. Any of the above

9. During a sales call, what do you usually think about?

A. Making the sale

B. Finding solutions to meet the customer's needs

C. Features and benefits of my product/service

10. If you could ask your prospects what they thought of you, what do you think they'd say?

A. Fun, likable, and easygoing

B. The jury is still out

C. Confident and competent

D. Not sure; I'm afraid to ask

Check for the answers to these questions in Appendix B.

How did you do? If you aced it, you're on the right track for making good first impressions. If you didn't, no worries; that's what we're here for. In Appendix B, you'll find detailed explanations for why each answer works to your advantage in creating good first impressions.

Quick Fix #2—The Handshake

Giving a proper handshake is crucial in any business or social interaction. How you shake hands can build or shatter your credibility, trustworthiness, and reputation. The following is a list of different types of handshakes and what they say about the people who give them.

YA DON'T SAY

Handshaking began when the ancient Romans clasped one another's arms to signal that they carried no weapons. The gesture was modified in medieval times when knights literally proved they had "nothing up their sleeves" by shaking hands. In the United States today, shaking hands is done as a signal of agreement, introduction, or welcome.

The CEO Handshake: For a handshake that communicates confidence and competence, the CEO is hard to beat. Reach out with thumb high, until the web between your thumb and forefinger connects with the same spot on the hand you are shaking. Wrap your hand firmly around the other four fingers, pressing your thumb into the fleshy part of the hand. Pump two or three times, while making eye contact and giving a warm, sincere smile.

With preliminaries out of the way and as you're giving your elevator speech, the gentleman you've been talking to leans forward, tilts his head, and nods. He gives you his card and asks you to set up an appointment with his assistant. Congratulations! The next two handshakes were made for such an occasion.

This handshake expresses confidence.

The Closer: To solidify a deal, glance up at your customer's eyes as you move in to shake; look down at the clasped hands to signal that you're on solid ground; then look up and seal the deal with a warm shoulder pat using your other hand. Works every time.

The Closer handshake helps you seal the deal.

The Thank You: When somebody pays you a compliment, or apologizes after a disagreement, the Thank You handshake is a great way to express sincere gratitude. In this handshake, you embrace the other person's hand with both of yours. This gesture, often accompanied by a smile or other emotional response, is also a great way for you to compliment or congratulate someone. It's a definite crowd pleaser.

A gracious handshake mends fences and expresses gratitude.

WORKIN' IT

It's always appropriate to shake hands as a colleague, customer, prospect, or guest exits. If you want to be remembered and make each feel validated, pump the hand two or three times, and as you begin to step away, maintain eye contact for a couple of seconds. This says, "I will never forget you." Powerful!

Just as handshakes can make great first impressions and seal the deal, there are also handshakes that will kill them. The following handshakes should be avoided at all costs:

The Wet Limp Fish: Imagine going hand-to-hand with a clammy, sticky, wet fish. Yuck! This handshake projects low self-esteem, neurosis, and anxiety. It can sabotage your best efforts.

Nothing kills a deal faster than a limp/wet handshake.

WORKIN' IT

A medical condition called *hyperhidrosis* causes uncontrollable sweating. If you tend to get wet, sticky palms, remember the old adage, "Never let them see you sweat." Spray your hands with antiperspirant in the morning, and wipe them discreetly on a napkin or handkerchief before extending your hand.

The Wimp: A lifeless handshake is sure to turn off potential prospects. Shake hands like this and you'll be perceived as weak, insecure, shy, and lacking authority.

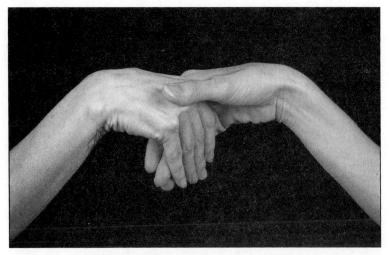

A lifeless handshake undermines your authority.

The Princess Grip: Unless you're royalty, this fingertip grip suggests prissiness and superiority. In business, any dainty, gentle gesture should be replaced with the confident CEO handshake.

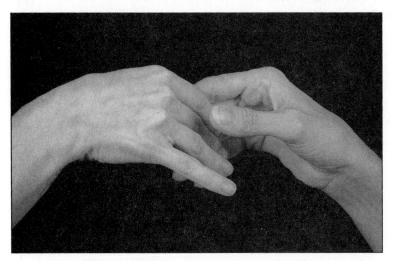

A fingertip grip comes across as prissy or haughty.

The Aggressor: We all know one of these—the kind of self-centered jerk who's always cutting in line at the grocery store. To an aggressor, your hand is a target. Before you can even extend your arm, they've snatched up your hand and wrung the life out of it. Aggressive, impatient, and presumptuous; avoid this one if you can help it.

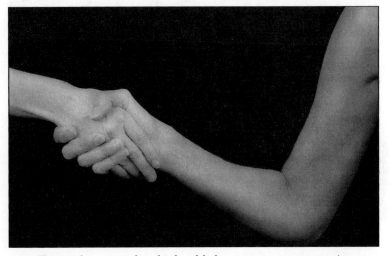

Turn it down a notch—this handshake comes across as aggressive.

The Dominator: Thumbs down on this gesture, unless you want to be perceived as a control freak. The dominator treats every handshake as a contest, coming in from above and pushing down with a hard squeeze. Also known as the Knuckle-Cruncher, the biggest impression this handshake leaves is in the poor victim's hand.

WORKIN' IT

To outmaneuver a dominator, take two steps forward, until you're side-by-side. During this maneuver, you slowly move your hand from horizontal to vertical, while maintaining a cordial shake. Finish with a couple of pats on the back. Now you've got the upper hand.

Shake it, don't break it.

Quick Fix #3—Eye Contact

Eye contact is critical, but where you focus your eyes is equally important. Here's a rule of thumb for good eye contact:

- 70 to 80 percent eye contact signals "You have my undivided attention."

- 50 to 70 percent signals "I'm not fully engaged."

- 50 percent or less signals "I'm disengaged."

- Defocused or glazed-over eyes signal "I'm bored."

- Dilated pupils signal arousal: "This is a great business deal," or "I'm physically attracted."

- Shifty eyes are perceived with suspicion, as if you are dodging the truth.

- Excessive eye blinking is perceived as anxiety or anticipation.

BODY BLOCK

Awkward staring (80 percent or more eye contact) can make people feel uncomfortable and is sometimes associated with stalking behavior. Break your gaze by looking away for a few seconds, and then return back to eye contact.

What you look at sends certain signals and is as telling as how long you look:

- Eyes focused on the tip of the nose to the corner of the eye is just right in business.

- Eyes focused on the mouth signal, "I am thinking about what it would be like to kiss you."

- Eyes focused below the chin signal, "I am thinking about the after 6:00 P.M. cocktail hour."

For a professional impression, keep your mind on business and your eyes on the upper face of the person you're chatting with.

Quick Fix #4—The Head Tilt

A slight lean of the head to the right or left, while maintaining eye contact, shows an active listener. When the tilt is held in a frozen position, it can indicate a conscious effort to appear to be listening, which may or may not be authentic.

Quick Fix #5—Head Nods

A man nods his head two or three times when he agrees with a specific fact or point. A woman tilts her head while bobbing it up and down, as if she is agreeable to anything and everything people say. This can appear weak, easily swayed, or lacking confidence.

BODY BLOCK

Women overuse head nods more often than men do. This can be perceived as submissiveness, rather than active listening, and may signal agreement to terms based on emotion, rather than logic.

Quick Fix #6—The Smile

A great smile is a people-magnet. Your genuine smile signals internal happiness and is associated with a positive outlook. We associate an infectious smile with people we can trust, and research has found that those who smile often are usually more generous and extroverted.

Quick Fix #7—Great Teeth

Fairly or not, poor oral hygiene is associated with low income and low social status. When you want to make a great first impression, or appear captivating and irresistible, beautiful white teeth are at the top of the list of "must haves." As proof, how many successful, high-income-earners do you know who have discolored teeth or gaping holes in their mouths?

Quick Fix #8—Walking Style

Your style and pace of walking reveal more than you think. Here are different walking styles and what they communicate:

Best Foot Forward is a quick pace with long strides that says you are confident, determined, courageous, and purposeful.

High Octane says "Watch out; I'm coming through." This express train walk will plow down anyone in its path. The fast walker is generally a type-A personality who wants to be the boss and in control.

Bigfoot is when you hear Sasquatch coming from down the hall. A persistent heavy footfall can make you seem stubborn or difficult to deal with.

Sluggard is like pulling your head along with your body like an old tugboat. The body barely moves; with each step, gravity seems to be pulling you backward. Best described as someone "dragging their feet" with effort. Sluggards are perceived as having low ambition or being laid back, lazy, sad, depressed, or uncertain.

Prancer is like a cat prowling down the hallway singing, "I'm too sexy for this place." Sashaying in a single file line, shifting one foot in front of the other, causing the hips to sway; this walk shouts, "Look at me!"

Stroller is a "walk in the park" attitude. The stroller likes to take in everything around them. The stop-and-go stride is often perceived as easily distracted and leisurely, with the attitude, "What's the hurry? We have all day."

Check out your walking stride in the mirror or ask a friend to tell you what yours looks like. Making adjustments to how you walk could give you a leg up in creating good first impressions.

Long strides display confidence.

Quick Fix #9—Posture

Surely you can still hear your mother's voice: "Stop slouching, and sit up straight." Mom was right. Take the string test—while standing, tie a string around the top button of your shirt or blouse, then tie the other end around the button on your slacks. Now sit down as you normally would. Is there any slack in the string? If so, your posture needs to be adjusted until the slack is removed.

When you sit down, avoid pushing your buttocks into the back of the seat. Try leaving 1 or 2 inches behind you, without forcing; stretch straight up, keeping your shoulders and buttocks balanced.

Good posture conveys power and poise. And studies have shown that the simple act of assuming a powerful pose releases testosterone—in both men and women. So in essence, you can even make a good impression on yourself.

Quick Fix #10—Open Gestures

To appear confident, competent, and trustworthy, avoid crossing your arms or ankles. Closed gestures such as crossing arms, legs, or feet are perceived as guarded, unapproachable, resistant, and deceptive. Rather, keep the center of your body open, whether seated or standing.

Also, avoid placing your briefcase, folders, handbags, or books in front of you in any face-to-face encounter, because this closes your body as well.

Keeping an open posture makes you appear approachable and trustworthy.

Pulling it all together, when your posture is open, your smile is bright, your stride is long, and your handshake is confident, you've used body language to your advantage. You can thank that prospective client for the opportunity, hold that eye contact for a couple of seconds, and turn to join the others, confident that you've made a good first impression.

The Least You Need to Know

- First impressions speak volumes and often never change.
- Walk, handshake, and posture reveal your personality.
- Active listening is communicated through how you hold your head and how you nod.
- Never look below someone's chin or at their lips; always focus on the tip of the nose to the corner of the eye.

Perception Is Reality

In This Chapter

- Judgment by your peers
- The messages your appearance is sending
- Clothing do's and don'ts
- The psychology of color

From shoes to tattoos, from clothes to facial hair, it all says something about you. Why shouldn't it? The way you groom, dress, and adorn your body are deliberate decisions that reflect your personality and character traits. When it comes to how others judge you and perceive you, these choices often speak louder than anything you say.

This chapter explores the various perceptions you create in others through the choices you make about your bodily appearance, who you're friends with, how you conduct yourself online, and more. You'll learn what these choices communicate and how they can affect you.

We, the Jury

When you open your mailbox and find that letter saying you've been summoned for jury duty, you have actually been summoned to the land of body language experts—and they will be reading yours like a book.

Actually, life is really no different than jury selection. It may not be as obvious, but opinions are being formed about others all day long in the workplace, in the classroom, in the neighborhood, at home, you name it.

You may be thinking during jury selection, "I'm not the one on trial here." But even a juror is judged—by the judge, the prosecutor, and the defense attorney—during jury selection. She's judged using the same visual cues you'll use, as a prospective juror, to form judgments about a defendant. What is she wearing? Who is she with? Does she look guilty? These are all things that will be assessed before the first shred of evidence has been presented.

Quite frankly, you *are* on trial, every day, everywhere, just like a defendant. It's not just a courtroom practice. You're being judged daily by a jury of your peers—employers, customers, and potential mates—based, to a large degree, on your outward appearance and the company you keep. But before you get too worried about that, realize that you're doing the same thing to others; it's just the way people are.

We are all being judged every day by a jury of our peers.

SAY WHAT?

Show me who a man's friends are, and I will tell you who he is.

—Ralph Waldo Emerson

Social networking has made "reading" other people easier than ever. Your "friends," your "likes," your entire life—if you allow it—can be seen by most anyone online.

More than 40 percent of employers say they conduct Internet searches on job applicants. And one third of all rejected applicants are eliminated on this factor alone. What happens in Vegas may stay in Vegas, but what happens online can follow you for life. I'm not just talking about that compromising picture of you from that wild night in college. Foul language, bad grammar, and seedy friends can hang you as well.

Dressing in a midriff-baring shirt can send the wrong impression to a potential employer.

Here's a philosophical question. If a picture is worth a thousand words, is a misleading picture as bad as a thousand lies?

When Angelina met Grant online, he hooked her by painting a picture of himself as a wealthy world traveler in his early 40s, looking for love and adventure on the high seas. In pictures, he was chiseled and tan, seated behind the wheel of a cabin cruiser, more yacht than fishing boat, sunlight glinting off his six-pack abs.

When Angelina met Grant for coffee, he was 10 years older, shorter—in both funds and stature—and much heavier than his profile persona. The boat? Borrowed. The tan? That was real. Being unemployed, Grant had lots of time to baste his ample belly at the beach. Needless to say, Angelina ordered her coffee to go.

The verdict on Grant was easy. But what about Angelina? Did she embellish her profile as well? Rounding up where the numbers were in her favor, and down by a year or a pound? Perhaps. People do it all the time.

The point is that mixed messages kill credibility, as was also demonstrated in Chapter 2. There's nothing wrong with making the most of what you have. But if you make a habit of embellishing the truth or making things up, the jury of life will throw the book at you. If you're lucky, it will be this book, so you can avoid making the same mistakes twice.

Case Clothed

You probably already know that the clothes you wear can tell other people a lot about your economic status and personality. There are also things that your clothing choices can tell you about yourself.

Take a lucky tie, for example, or any clothes you wear as much for luck as for the way they look. Researchers at Northwestern University have determined that the "luck" in such talismans is real. As it turns out, luck has less to do with the clothes themselves than the way those clothes make you feel when you're wearing them. The Northwestern study found that students presented with identical white coats to wear performed at different levels, depending on whether the coat they received was described as a painter's smock or a doctor's lab coat.

Participants in the lab coat group reported a higher level of attentiveness than the group in the smocks. This "smart clothes" phenomenon is known as *enclothed cognition*.

SAY WHAT?

Enclothed cognition is the systematic influence that clothes have on the wearer's psychological processes.

"Smart clothes" such as a lab coat can have a profound influence on how you feel about yourself.

Clothes Audit

Your answers to the following questions will help you as you read on about the role of clothes in body language.

Ask yourself the following:

- When was the last time I went shopping for clothes, shoes, a briefcase, or a handbag?

- When was the last time someone complimented my clothes?

- Is my closet filled with clothes of various sizes?

- How many items in my closet still have price tags on them?

- When was the last time I purged my closet of old and outdated clothes?

If your clothes are going to talk to you and about you, you may want to get rid of the ones that don't have anything nice to say, such as:

- Does your closet scream "out of date"? A reluctance to part with outdated clothes could signal resistance to change, or outdated thinking. And don't even think about using that old "vintage" hedge. If you're old enough to have worn something when it was first in fashion, you're too old to make it work the second time around.

- Are there clothes with the tags still on them months, or years, after the purchase? Emotional purchases are the clothing equivalent of eating a whole quart of ice cream. Don't wallow in guilt. Let them go.

- Do you have clothes in various sizes? These ghosts of glory days gone by only serve to point up your shortcomings. Why hang onto something that doesn't make you feel good *now?* Rule of thumb: if you haven't worn something in a year, donate it to charity.

Get rid of clothes that are outdated and don't make you feel good.

Now that you understand the closet, let's build your wardrobe back up with a look that will communicate confidence, leadership, power, and success—to yourself, as well as to others.

Ten Clothing Must-Haves for Women

- Black dress. It means leadership and power, and you will always have an occasion for a black dress. (Add a splash of color with a scarf or broach.)

- Black, navy, or gray two-piece pantsuit. It says sophisticated and professional, a great mix and match.

- Black, navy, or charcoal blazer. It is timeless and professional.

- Black straight skirt. It screams sophisticated, professional, and feminine, when mixed with a colorful blouse.

- Solid-colored pants or dress jeans. These communicate casual, confident style. Top them with a fun jacket.

- A nice black or white solid top/blouse. These go with anything. Add more colors as you continue building your wardrobe.

- Black, closed-toed leather pumps. These say confidence. Up to a 3-inch heel, depending on your height.

- Diamond studs and pearls. Simplicity is key. Simply displayed diamonds and pearls convey confidence, elegance, intelligence, and success.

- Classic handbag and briefcase—black or tobacco brown. A leather briefcase has long stood for authority and success. Classic looks suggest position and power.

- Up-to-date haircut worn above the shoulders or pulled up. Short hair says, "I am in control of my appearance and confident in myself and what I represent."

On the other hand, when tops are too tight or too low-cut, heels are more than 4 inches, dresses are slinky, clothes are wrinkled or stained, shoes are scuffed, or heels are torn, the perception is typically not in good favor. The assessment can be if you can't pull yourself together, you may not be trusted to get the job done, whether it's in the workplace, in the jury box, or elsewhere.

Ideal work attire for women.

Ten Clothing Must-Haves for Men

- Two to four suits. One black and others in either tan or brown, charcoal, or navy pin-stripe. Quality counts. A good fit and a good fabric say, "I know what I'm doing."

- Black, brown, or burgundy lace-up shoes. Again, nothing fancy. But keep a shine on those shoes, and get to know a good cobbler. Shabby shoes say, "I don't pay attention to detail."

- Five high-quality white shirts. Make sure the shirts are professionally dry-cleaned and slightly starched, with a nice texture. It projects substance and professionalism.

- Three belts, one each of black, brown, and burgundy. No deep meaning here. You've got to match your shoes, and keep your pants up.

- Variety of colored shirts and ties (don't forget pink; it's the new power color for men). Not too bold—a little color goes a long way.

- Nice cufflinks, newer leather wallet, and well-kept black/brown leather or metal briefcase. Attention to detail in dress demonstrates that you've got your world in order.

- A nice watch. It suggests you appreciate fine things, and can be counted on to keep to a schedule.

- Neutral-colored trench coat. Not a lot of options in this area—more of a practical necessity.

- Blue, black, brown, and tan socks. Socks should match your pants.

- Twelve cotton t-shirts. Or enough to get you through between laundry days.

- Bonus—a black cashmere blazer. A luxury, but one that speaks of wealth and position.

For men, pants that are too long or too short, scuffed shoes, outdated suits, polyester colored suits and short coats, suspenders (unless you are Larry King), unmatched socks, neckties that are too short or too long, a cheap watch, or an old wallet are things that don't bode well for communicating confidence and competence.

Left: Ideal male work attire. Right: Even with the right attire, sloppy attention to detail can come across as unprofessional.

Sole Searching

Don't think shoes have much to say? Then why do so many have tongues? A University of Kansas study, published in 2012, sparked widespread debate about the psychology of shoe selection. The study itself, which included such revelations as the fact that people who wore masculine shoes tended to be men, wasn't as remarkable as the attention it generated.

This topic is important to consider, however, if only to illustrate how reasonable people can interpret identical data differently, and underscore the previous point that context is key in reading nonverbal cues.

For example, depending on who you ask …

- High-top sneakers are either for introverts with *attachment anxiety* or artsy extroverts who bask in attention.

> **SAY WHAT?**
>
> **Attachment anxiety** is when a person has a fear of abandonment or rejection.

- Old, shabby shoes are favored by both rich world travelers and homeless people.

- New, expensive shoes are a sign of either wealth or a personality disorder.

- People who take good care of their shoes are either neurotics overly concerned with what other people think, or just people who take good care of their stuff.

- Ankle boots are either for aggressive or fun people.

- Uncomfortable shoes are worn by calm people, although, why would anyone intentionally wear uncomfortable shoes—and how could you tell, as an observer?

- Flip-flops are for hippies, or middle-class fathers of four on vacation.

The bottom line is that while shoe style and condition may help to reinforce your assessment of someone, shoes alone aren't basis enough to form conclusive opinions. Remember: Context matters.

Different styles of shoes, based on context, can provide information about the personality of the wearer.

Looks *Do* Matter

Beauty may be only skin deep, but that's all anyone can see at first glance, so, like it or not, physically attractive people actually do make a better first impression. It may not seem fair, but again, it's just how people are.

YA DON'T SAY

According to Kevin Hogan, PsyD, author of *The Psychology of Persuasion*, people who are considered more attractive make more money, are promoted more quickly, are favored by teachers, get better grades in school, are treated better, have more opportunities, get more dates, and get off with a lighter sentence than those who are considered less attractive.

Research says that 61 percent of humans are visually oriented, which means that they form their opinions primarily by what they observe. Your physical appearance sends a nonverbal message of your social status, character, income, intelligence, competence, and confidence.

Yes, beauty is in the eye of the beholder, but attractive people are at a distinct advantage. The good news is there are a few adjustments anyone can make to become more attractive. We already covered clothing, so let's explore a few others.

Hairstyle

Ask any hair stylist—they know. They can detect when a customer is getting divorced, having an affair, getting a promotion, seeking attention, feeling promiscuous, stuck in the past, depressed, having a mid-life crisis, okay with themselves, or stuck in hum-drum mode. Hairstyle is an indicator of what's happening in someone's life—and in their head. Let's look at what's going on inside these heads:

Dramatic changes in style suggest big changes in life.

Facial Hair

Facial hair no longer carries the same stigma as in the past; in fact, it can spruce you up and give you a fashion-forward appeal. Statistics do show, however, that clean-shaven professionals generally rank higher in position than those with facial hair. So if you're an aspiring CEO or executive, clean-shaven is best.

Facial hair adds three to six years to your perceived age, so if you're looking to appear a little older, a well-groomed beard may work to your advantage.

The statistics on the pros and cons of facial hair are, well, fuzzy. One thing, however, is certain: a scruffy, unkempt beard is associated with uncleanliness and sloth, and can have a negative effect.

Tattoos

While ink is certainly in, it needs to stay in, meaning covered up by clothing. It's your body, do what you want; but when ink is out (that is, where other people—particularly prospective employers and clients—can see it), you've got a perception problem.

It doesn't matter whether it's a purple unicorn or a big ole heart with a banner that says "Mom," studies show that visible tattoos lower your credibility and can repel opportunities. In the dating world, people tend to perceive women with large, visible tattoos as less intelligent, more dishonest, and more promiscuous.

Tattoos should be covered in the work environment.

Piercings

Body modification is a growing art form expressed by men and women among all socio-economic cultures. Despite its popularity among well-educated professionals, "bod-mod" carries a stigma associated with rebellion. In the workplace, professionals admit that they cover visible modifications during meetings and special events. Because of the stigma attached, piercings may inhibit career opportunities.

Interesting Facts About Appearance

What we wear and how we look speak volumes about who we are, how we feel about ourselves, what we value, and what we want to achieve at any given time. While most people have an innate ability to pick up on these silent messages, the key is being able to accurately read and interpret them.

The following list is a handy summary of many of the concepts we've discussed in this chapter concerning appearance:

1. We trust that what we see on the surface is an accurate echo of what lies beneath.

2. Our total appearance and grooming speak to the world about who we are.

3. There is no such thing as dressing in a neutral way.

4. How you dress or act will create your reality.

5. What one wears is assumed to reflect characteristics, attributes, and attitudes of the wearer.

6. Anyone dressed as a known stereotype will be assumed to have the same character traits.

7. First impressions attract or repel opportunities.

8. Our clothes and grooming affect how we think, feel, and behave.

9. Most people only notice extremes.

10. Friends who dress alike are more critical of those dressing in a different manner.

11. Those consumed by their own appearance are judgmental about others' appearances.

12. Wearing clothes and accessories that match will intensify the mood.

13. Attractive people get greater opportunities in life than those who are unattractive.

14. Appropriateness and respect are the most important aspects of appearance.

15. Dress reflects character, beliefs, values, status, role, lifestyle, and attributes.

(List courtesy of Ann Reinten, President, Image Innovators—Australia)

Color Psychology

Have you ever wondered why you feel more comfortable in green rooms than red, or why you eat more in red rooms? That's because color affects our moods and attitudes. So you can imagine how certain clothing colors can affect the way others feel about you and the opinions you form about them.

> **WORKIN' IT**
>
> Think color first when selecting your clothing for an event. Match the clothing to the mood that is appropriate.

Let's explore different colors and what they communicate:

- **Black.** This color gets a bad rap because it is favored by goths and cartoon villains. The truth is, these groups wear black for the same reason you should—it's the color of power, control, and authority. (It can make you look thinner, too!)

- **White.** The color of angels, scientists, and health-care professionals, white connotes innocence, purity, and sterility.

- **Red.** The color of love and passion, this impish hue provokes powerful emotions. Red can be seen as confrontational, so it's probably not the best color to wear to a negotiation. In dating, red is seen as a "fast" color, particularly on women.

- **Blue.** Peaceful, serene, and tranquil, blue means business. Although blue is the color we associate with sadness, studies have shown it to evoke both trust and loyalty. It's a great color for interviews.

- **Green.** Calming, refreshing, and relaxing, green is also the color of money. For men, a dark green signifies masculinity, wealth, and conservatism.

- **Yellow.** Attention grabber and optimistic, yellow demands attention and promotes concentration. A good color for public speakers, except for politicians, it is a hot color associated with provocation and anger.

- **Purple.** The color of royalty, luxury, and sophistication, purple is a playful color that can suggest everything from empathy to self-indulgence. A little purple goes a long way, with lighter shades conveying confidence, while darker and bolder shades may appear artificial or contrived.

- **Brown.** A humble, solid color, brown signals genuineness and conservatism. A common color for men's suits, this color is all business. It's definitely not a playful color.

In 2003, Joe Hallock, a student at the University of Washington, conducted an online survey to determine the "color" of various emotions—trust, quality, desperation, etc. The results for colors associated with "trust" help quantify what those of us in the image-consulting business have been saying for some time—namely that blue is called "true blue" for a reason. Here are the results:

- 34 percent blue
- 21 percent white
- 11 percent green
- 8 percent purple
- 7 percent yellow
- 6 percent red
- 4 percent black, brown, and grey
- 1 percent orange

We said earlier that black is the color of power and authority. Let's break that down a little further. It turns out, the deeper the black, the more power. That's why most successful executives wear black, charcoal, or blue-black/deep navy.

A black suitcoat and black-framed glasses give an impression of authority.

WORKIN' IT

For a look that both conveys power and establishes trust, wear shades of blue, white, or green in shirts, ties, tops, or broaches. Wear them under black, brown, or grey suits. One exception is in job interviews where it can work to your advantage to subtly wear the company's colors.

The Least You Need to Know

- Your appearance speaks volumes about you.
- Your shoes reflect your personality traits.
- Facial hair, tattoos, and piercings are often judged unfavorably by others.
- Color has psychological effects on you and others.

Face Time

In This Chapter

- How to read facial expressions with accuracy
- How expressions reveal our true emotions
- How to understand smiles, eye contact, and head movement

You're in love, and the whole world knows it. You and your beloved can't wipe the smiles from your faces. Those frozen-in-place grins stretch from ear to ear, exposing every last molar. And oh my, those goo-goo eyes! Love is written all over your faces because facial expressions are a direct product of our emotions.

Face-reading is one of the key ways to understand other human beings. We interpret people based on their words, their voices, their body language, and their expressions. But facial expressions are the most reliable gauge of true feelings.

Facial expressions are like a personal tattle-tale riding on your shoulder, always ready to trumpet your true thoughts, no matter how hard you might try to conceal them. Every one of us has thoughts and feelings we might not want to share with the world. But they leak out no matter how hard we try to repress them, like steam from a hot kettle, in micro-expressions for everyone to see.

The Seven Universal Facial Expressions of Emotions

Many facial expressions are involuntary, not intentional. And they are universal. Traveling around the globe and photographing people from every culture, Dr. Paul Ekman, psychologist and world leader in the field of facial expressions, proved that people everywhere, and in every time, experience seven universal facial expressions of emotions. The expressions that show in all human faces in the same way are:

- Anger
- Contempt
- Disgust
- Fear

- Happiness
- Sadness
- Surprise

YA DON'T SAY

Faces don't lie. A trained observer can correctly identify another's emotions 96 percent of the time, based solely on facial expression.

Can You Read Faces?

Face-reading is like putting a puzzle together. With each piece, the picture becomes clearer. Before we teach you to recognize these seven emotions, take the following quiz to discover your innate face-reading skills. Select an expression and match it to an emotion in the following list.

Give yourself no more than one minute to complete the quiz. In real life, these expressions can come and go in the blink of an eye, so it is important to recognize them quickly.

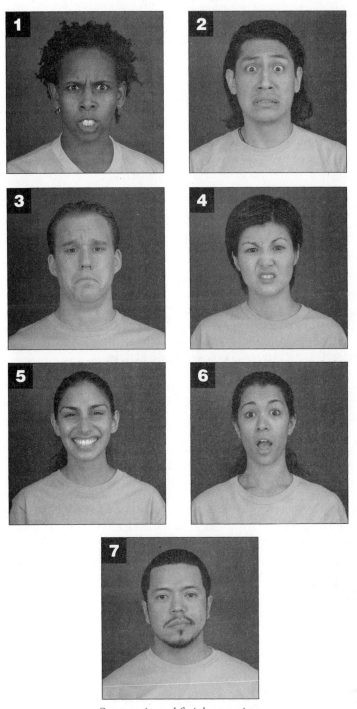

Seven universal facial expressions.
(Copyright Dr. David Matsumoto)

Check your answers in Appendix B. If the number you got right is …

- 7—Congratulations! You're already a pro.
- 6—You're above the average Joe.
- 5—You're just about right.
- Below 5—You're a work in progress.

Don't worry if you were not sure about a few of the expressions or were even flat-out wrong. Without training, most people judge facial expressions correctly only 50 percent of the time. This holds true even among clinical psychologists, judges, and police officers. It takes training to truly read a face.

It's no wonder that face-reading requires training; there are more than 40 muscles in the face that respond to our emotions. These muscles, by themselves and in combination with others, create a limitless number of facial expressions.

Some Reactions Are Predictable

Here's a scenario: You're walking to your car at the neighborhood grocery store on a sunny afternoon. Someone taps you on the shoulder from behind. Your eyes open wide, your eyebrows pull straight up, and your mouth drops open.

You can't help it. All of these facial movements are involuntary. And that particular combination, according to Ekman, indicates surprise.

Now imagine it's late at night, in a dark, remote parking lot when that tap comes on your shoulder. Based on Ekman's research documenting expressions of fear, we can predict with some certainty that your eyes would open even wider—to a position we call a "three-corner white," in which the whites of the eye show on both sides and above the iris. Your mouth might drop slightly, but it would definitely tighten and stretch toward your ears. This is an expression of fear.

BODY BLOCK

Reading faces provides insight into intentions, motivations, credibility, and trustworthiness. But keep your ears open, too. If someone's words and facial expressions don't match, be wary.

Mirror, Mirror on the Wall

Body language is a two-way street. If you can't read yourself, how can you expect to read others? Understand what the seven universal expressions of emotions look like on your own face, and, more importantly, know what they feel like.

Here are exercises to deepen your knowledge of our universal expressions of emotions.

Place a mirror in front of you. Read the following characteristics of each emotion. Try to contort the muscles in your face to create the expression. Be conscious of every little muscle movement in your face. Feel how the muscles strain against a normal, relaxed state. Begin with surprise and move down the list as you master each one.

This creates an expression of surprise:

> Think of a time you felt surprised.
>
> Begin by lifting your eyebrows vertically.
>
> Now open your eyes, wide.
>
> Now drop your bottom jaw.

An expression of surprise.

This creates an expression of disgust:

> Recall a foul odor.
>
> Begin by lifting your upper lip on one or both sides.
>
> Scrunch up your nose vertically until your nose wrinkles.
>
> Now narrow and squint your eyes.

An expression of disgust.

This creates an expression of contempt:

> Think about a time you felt superior.
>
> Close your lips together in a natural position.
>
> Now move one side of your mouth horizontally toward your ear.
>
> Optional: Tilt your head back slightly.

An expression of contempt.

This creates an expression of sadness:

> Think about a sad moment.
>
> Pull the inner corners of your eyebrows toward each other.
>
> Allow your upper eyelids to drop and your eyes to defocus.
>
> Now turn the outer corners of your mouth down and pout your chin.

An expression of sadness.

This creates an expression of happiness:

> Think about a time you experienced joy.
>
> Raise both corners of your mouth up toward your cheeks.
>
> Now lift your cheeks up toward your eyes.
>
> Notice the crow's feet around your eyes.
>
> Your mouth may open or remain closed.

An expression of happiness.

This creates an expression of fear:

> Think of a scary moment.
>
> Raise your top eyelids up high until the whites above your eyes appear.
>
> Now stretch both sides of your mouth horizontally toward your ears.
>
> Your lower jaw may or may not drop slightly.

An expression of fear.

This creates an expression of anger:

> Think of a time you felt angry.
>
> Lower your eyebrows and pull them inward.
>
> Now narrow your eyes.
>
> Glare intensely from your eyes.
>
> Press your lips together and pull them inward.

An expression of anger.

As you worked your way through this exercise, did you notice that you began to feel the emotion you were trying to reflect in your face? Research has found that you can change your mood by changing your facial expression. Remember your mother's admonition to wipe that frown off your face and put on a smile? She intuitively knew that acting happy would make it so. If you don't feel on top of your game, do a mirror-check.

Make a conscious effort to present to the world the facial expressions that align with the person you want to be. Pretty soon, you will be that person, and effortlessly radiate a positive message that will attract others in your business and personal relationships.

> **YA DON'T SAY**
>
> Psychologists at Princeton University found that we size up each other in the blink of an eye, making snap but lasting judgments in as little as 100 milliseconds. Equally as fast are some telling facial expressions which flash on and off so quickly that untrained observers are not consciously aware of what has transpired.

Faces Reveal Competency

Look at the following two photos for five seconds. Think of five reasons why one person appears more competent than the other.

Whom would you hire?

Did you find yourself picking one person apart more than the other? Maybe you think one person's nose is too big, or one's eyes are beady, or one strikes you as a shyster. Or maybe you don't like a hairstyle or think one person looks smug. This exercise is about perception, first impressions, and subjective feelings.

But that's not what professional facial expression analysis is about. Reading facial expressions is not about judging someone's character. The goal of a professional analysis is to determine someone's emotional state from an objective interpretation of muscle movement backed by scientific research.

Tricks of the Trade

Most of the facial expressions we've been discussing are involuntary muscle movements. But as we've seen, facial expressions can be intentional. Earlier in this chapter you practiced moving your facial muscles to create a particular facial expression and feeling how the expression can begin to change your mood. There's another way that intentional facial expressions can be used purposefully to great advantage in your personal and business relationships.

The Eyebrow Flash

This is a very quick movement in which you raise your eyebrows straight up and then quickly release them. If you do it correctly, you will feel the center muscle in your forehead lift. This movement signals interest. This is a flash, not a frozen expression. You don't want to scare anyone. A quick eyebrow flash can also be employed to emphasize a point.

Eyebrows locked in the upright position can be used to intimidate or as a reprimand. Have you ever seen someone raise their eyebrows as they peer over the top of their glasses? This is most often seen in people in power, such as judges, bosses, or parents standing their ground.

A quick raise of the eyebrows expresses interest.

The Head Tilt and Nod

The head tilt needs no further description. It's an active listening gesture that comes naturally to someone engaged in a conversation. Leaning your head to one side signals to the speaker, "I am interested in what you are saying."

Tilting the head slightly shows you are actively listening to what the other person is saying.

WORKIN' IT

Don't overuse the head tilt. Ladies, more than men, tend to overuse the head tilt. When she holds her head in the tilted position for too long, a lady can appear submissive and lacking in confidence.

Head nods show you agree or affirm what the other person is saying. This should be done in moderation. Three to four pumps is plenty to get your point across. Overusing nods can make you appear as if you are agreeable to everything. Try to avoid looking like a dashboard bobblehead.

The late Princess Diana's demure look melted men's hearts. To pull it off, ladies, tilt your head down at an angle, dropping your chin an inch or two. At the same time, glance up with just your eyes. Look him square in the eye, and watch him react to the goosebumps running up his spine! Men can try this, too. It has the same effect on the ladies!

Channel Princess Diana's grace with this look.

The Lip Pump

This is a funny gesture that primates unconsciously do when they are attracted to each other. But the lip pump also can be used more intentionally, to great effect, by humans. The lip pump is triggered by looking at another's mouth and wondering how it would feel to kiss those lips. The lips pump, or pout, as if they are puckering up for a kiss.

The lip pump indicates attraction.

Real Smile, or Crocodile?

Smiles have many meanings and interpretations. A genuine smile produces the characteristics of happiness as described earlier in this chapter. The lips curl up, the cheeks raise, and the eyes narrow, creating crow's feet in the corners. But not all smiles are true.

You run into a business acquaintance on the street. After a brief conversation, he says, "Let's get together soon for a drink. I'll call you." Big smile. Big handshake. But you never hear from him again. Maybe that surprised you, but it shouldn't. Deceptive people often hide behind a smile. The smile might be followed by a giggle or a laugh. Haven't you heard these phrases before?

- "I really didn't mean that!"
- "I would never do that!"
- "I think you look great!"

A genuine smile.

A false smile.

A cordial smile.

A critical or condescending smile.

The Smirk

This is the scornful smile of contempt. It appears as a half-smile, with one side of the mouth pulling horizontally toward the ear. The smirk sometimes gets confused with a genuine smile, but it is insincere. You will see this expression in the midst of a conversation when a listener who feels superior and disagrees with the speaker is thinking to himself, "You don't know the facts; you don't have a clue; I know more than you. I'm more intelligent than you; you're a jerk." The feeling of superiority leaks out in a smirk.

You're full of it!

The Smug

The smug or condescending smile is like the smirk, except that the smiler additionally brings an attitude of self-righteousness. This expression is seen when the upper lip presses down on the lower lip and tightens while the outside corners of the mouth turn up as if to say, "I don't believe a word you are saying, really!" The smug smile can be accompanied by a raised eyebrow, the head leaning back, nose up in the air, or a sideways look. The smirk and smug expressions can be interrelated; both are demeaning expressions that, if noticed, will make the target feel inferior.

A smug look conveys self-righteousness.

Raising Your Eye-Q

Eye contact is an essential part of communication. When you speak face-to-face, the appropriate amount of time to "lock eyes" is 70 to 80 percent. Anything more starts to feel creepy. But much less eye contact suggests you are bored, distracted, uninterested, or just plain rude. If someone is interested in what you have to say, their eyes will be on you, not darting around the room, watching other people walking by, or checking their phone. And while you're making eye contact, take note of these other eye cues.

Appropriate eye contact indicates genuine interest.

Revealing Pupils

Have you ever seen a professional poker player wearing sunglasses? A good hand in a tense game triggers feelings of arousal that can be reflected in the eyes. That's what card players call a "tell" and it's something a smart player may take steps to hide, behind their shades, from their competitors.

Anatomically speaking, the purpose of the pupil in your eye is to regulate the amount of light entering the retina. But pupils also react to emotions. The wider the pupils, the greater the emotion. Like a good hand at the poker table, a physical attraction or a profitable business transaction can generate feelings of anticipation, excitement, and arousal that are revealed in the size of the pupils.

YA DON'T SAY

Magazine stylists often alter models' eyes in photos to make them appear dilated, because dilated eyes are beguiling at a subliminal level. Blue eyes are particularly provocative because of their strong contrast with a wide black pupil.

The Eye Pull

Unless it's allergy season and you're observing someone with dry, itchy eyes, watch out for the eye pull. Someone who tugs at the outer corner of one eye, pulling the corner horizontally toward the ear, is showing contempt. The eye puller might be in the process of boasting, exaggerating, or trying to deceive you.

This eye pull is a boasting signal.

Avoidance

If someone otherwise makes good eye contact with you, take note of what is being discussed when their eyes dart off to the left or right. This is a suspicious and reliable sign of avoidance. Darting eyes don't necessarily mean the person is lying, but rather that the topic of conversation causes discomfort for some reason.

Darting eyes can signal avoidance.

Field Trip

Now that you know what to look for, let's visit some friends in the following scenarios for a little "face" time.

When Claudia Met Paul

Two years after his divorce, Paul met Claudia through an online dating service. The two chatted via email for three months, building what Paul thought was the beginning of a potentially lasting relationship with a woman who seemed open and attentive to his feelings. Paul was nervous when they finally met face-to-face, because he knew he no longer looked exactly like the outdated photo on his online profile. As Claudia saw Paul for the first time, her reaction was not unexpected. Her smile seemed forced and strained.

For a brief moment, the muscles in her eyebrows pulled together, wrinkling her forehead. Claudia's facial expressions were clear indicators of distress from disappointment. The date, unfortunately, did not have a fairytale ending. But Paul took to heart the moral of the story: a "current" photo means one taken within at least the past decade.

Overwhelmed with Joy

Heather and Blake, first-time parents, seemed to overflow with feelings of love at the birth of little Madison. As soon as the umbilical cord was cut, the nurse placed the newborn baby on Heather's tummy. To Heather's surprise, Blake's chin began to quiver. His mouth dropped, and tears welled up in his eyes. Blake's facial expression was a classic example of someone flooded by emotion—in his case, joy—whose true feelings could be easily misinterpreted, if observed out of context.

Power Play

Handsome and sophisticated, Bill swept Joan off her feet. Their romance was intense, but short-lived. In the midst of the affair, Joan lent Bill $12,000 to buy a used car, trusting that either they would be together forever, or that he would honorably repay her. Alas, Joan's trust was misplaced, and she and Bill wound up before a court mediator in a fight over the debt. Over an hour of back-and-forth negotiation, Bill unsuccessfully tried to manipulate and intimidate Joan in several different ways. Facing a full-blown trial, both agreed to sign a joint stipulation in which Bill promised to repay Joan $500 a month until the debt was cleared.

Joan felt relieved, but only because she failed to read a crucial but important micro-expression on Bill's face. As they shook on the deal, Bill smirked, the left side of his mouth shifting slightly and briefly toward his ear. It was a sign of contempt and the pleasure he took in duping her, because Bill knew at that moment that he would be filing for bankruptcy, where his debt to Joan would be erased. Sadly, had Joan known how to read facial expressions, she would have been warned.

Even a Nonexpression Is an Expression

Expressionless, void and empty, the stone face is an expression in and of itself. It's a look that's often intentional, hard, and intimidating for others to read. For good reason, the stone face also is known as the poker face.

Once again, serious card players who study each other to gain advantage in the game become skilled at blocking all visible cues. A stone face can be worn effectively by people who are expected to remain objective (such as judges, police officers, and journalists). But in personal relationships, a stone face can prevent intimacy.

When you hide your feelings behind a stone face, out of fear of rejection, you give up the chance to have your love requited. A stone face also can be a sign of a psychological disorder.

The stone face shuts out others.

Now that you know what facial expressions look and feel like, apply your new knowledge to everyday life experiences. With practice, you will begin to sharpen your skills. Always remember the caveat that no one expression tells the whole story—you can recognize the emotion but still not know its context.

The Least You Need to Know

- The face reveals authentic emotions.
- Faces hold the most reliable sources for reading people.
- Smiles can reveal anything from genuine joy to bitter contempt.
- Pupils dilate when a person is feeling anxiety or excitement.

How People Learn and Communicate

In This Chapter

- Learning the three styles of communication and learning
- Discovering your personal style
- Becoming a persuasive communicator

Understanding how people learn and communicate is important, not only for what it says about them, but also for the power it gives you to persuade and influence them.

Ever wondered how television evangelists, motivational speakers, and sales professionals persuade you to take action? You'll find out in this chapter how persuasive communication is, not just the words that are said, but how they are said and how they connect to you. This chapter explores the three styles of learning and communicating and how they will help you in your interactions with others.

Styles of Learning

Everyone has a primary, dominant style of learning and communication. For example, one customer may prefer to see a product before purchasing it; another may want to hear about it over the phone, or hear you talk about its features and benefits; and there are always those who would prefer to test-drive a product before purchasing it. Those who make it their business to study such things call these three styles visual, auditory, and kinesthetic, respectively—VAK for short. Surveys suggest that, as a whole, the learning styles of the general public look like the following.

Visual (seeing)
61 percent

Auditory (hearing)
18.5 percent

Kinesthetic (feeling)
20.5 percent

How to Read Learning Styles Through Body Language

As you've probably guessed, body language can tell you a lot about someone's dominant learning style. Let's explore what that language looks like for each style.

Visual Body Language

Visual learners and communicators typically have the following characteristics to their body language:

- Fast-paced walkers
- Rapid speech and higher pitch when excited
- Easily distracted
- Expansive hand gestures, outside body frame
- Eyes dart/flit when talking
- Breathe high in the chest, rapid and shallow
- Eyes look up to recall an event

The body language of a visual learner.

YA DON'T SAY

Visual communicators learn by observing—seeing pictures, maps, graphs, and visual aids.

Auditory Body Language

Auditory learners and communicators typically have the following characteristics to their body language:

- Articulate punctuation of words
- Good speakers
- May tilt head to the side when communicating one-on-one
- A voice that resonates
- Breathing is in mid-chest
- Eyes may look to the right or left when recalling an event

The body language of an auditory learner.

YA DON'T SAY

Auditory communicators learn by listening. They learn by hearing and speaking with others. In order to understand and retain information, they must clearly hear what's been said.

Kinesthetic Body Language

Kinesthetic learners and communicators typically have the following characteristics to their body language:

- Slower-paced walk
- Breathe deeply and may sigh
- Speak slower, softer; may draw words out
- May wrap arms around their body—snuggles
- Calm, emotional, and caring

- Eyes may look down when talking; may slump
- Touch others when talking
- Stand closer to others
- Like to huddle in groups

The body language of a kinesthetic learner.

WORKIN' IT

Kinesthetic communicators learn through experiencing and through touch.

What Style Are You?

Let's see where you fall in the learning style spectrum. The following quizzes will give an idea of your style. Simply answer yes or no to the following questions on a separate piece of paper.

Visual

1. Do you learn best through graphs, illustrations, or charts?

2. Before going to the store, do you make out a list, and then check off items in the store?

3. Do you find yourself speaking faster than others and become frustrated with those who can't keep up?

4. Are you suspicious of others who avoid or are unable to maintain eye contact during a conversation?

5. If you were in a court of law as a juror, would you have to see the evidence to believe it?

6. When you go into another's home, does it say something about their cleanliness?

7. When developing a concept, do you see the end result in mind?

8. When talking to others, do you use your hands a lot to illustrate your points?

9. When people talk a lot, does it get on your nerves?

10. On vacation, do you prefer to take in the town by yourself, instead of taking a guided tour?

Auditory

1. When you read directions, do you often speak them out loud?

2. Do you get aggravated when another person doesn't punctuate a word correctly, and do you correct them on the spot?

3. Do you prefer listening to music over watching television?

4. When communicating with others, do you often acknowledge the other person verbally by saying "I hear what you're saying"?

5. Do you often repeat a point so the other person gets it?

6. Are you ever accused of talking too much or rambling on?

7. Can you remember most of the words in a song and sing along with the radio?

8. Do you recall conversations in detail?

9. Do you find yourself getting annoyed or uncomfortable when others become emotional?

10. Can you maintain your concentration while others are talking?

Kinesthetic

1. Do you prefer to look at the picture and go for it when putting something together, instead of reading the directions?

2. Do you like to garden?

3. When meeting people, do you have the urge to give them a hug?

4. When someone shakes your hand, do you find yourself shaking back with both of your hands?

5. Do you get emotional when watching a poignant story?

6. Do you find yourself saying "I understand what you're saying," or "I understand how you feel," rather than "I see your point?"

7. Do you get irritated when others talk too fast or cut conversations short?

8. Do you tend to buy a car for the way it feels when you're driving it, rather than the stylish way it looks?

9. Do you go on vacations to the same places each year?

10. On the weekends do you like having people over—the more the merrier?

Tally up your answers in each style, keeping in mind that anything higher than six in one or more categories indicates your dominant learning style.

Did you find you were close in two categories or very strong in one main category? If you were clearly stronger in one category, this is where you live mostly, but you may visit in others. For example, your primary learning and communication style may be visual, but you visit occasionally in auditory or kinesthetic.

This is a great test to share with colleagues, employees, or significant others. The more you know, collectively, about your individual learning styles, the better you'll function as a group.

Apply What You've Learned

Learning styles and body language work together effortlessly. A person will undoubtedly communicate their learning style and level of interest in the subject at hand through simple body gestures you've learned about thus far.

Let's look at some examples of how this works out in the world. To simplify the speakers' identities in the dialogue, I will refer to "K" for the kinesthetic customer, and "V" for the visual salesperson.

The following scenario is about a customer who wants to buy lawn furniture.

Take 1

V: Hello, may I help you?

K: Yes, I'm shopping for lawn furniture to seat six to eight people. I've got some out-of-town guests coming this weekend, and I want them to be comfortable.

V: I think we have what you're looking for. This beautiful teakwood set was hand-crafted in Miami. The bright color combination would look stunning on your back porch or pool deck.

K: I was thinking of something more homey and comfortable. All those colors make me nervous. I don't want to show off; I just want my guests to feel at home.

V: Did you have a price range in mind?

K: Well, I feel like I'd want something that's going to last.

V: Okay, let me show you a set that sells like hotcakes. We can't even keep 'em in stock, the way they fly out the door!

K: I don't care for this set; it feels uncomfortable. My back sits straight up. I want something my guests can relax and sprawl out on. Let me come back another time, when you get something new in.

V: Okay, here's my card. Please ask for me when you come back in.

K: Will do.

In this scenario, the salesperson failed to read that the customer's dominant learning style was kinesthetic. The customer was not interested in the furniture's construction, its color, or where it was manufactured. Out of exasperation, she gave up and said she would return at another time.

Do you think she would return? Not likely; she said her need was immediate. But if she did, chances are that she would ask for a different salesperson. It seems the salesperson was more interested in showing his taste than reading and fulfilling the customer's need.

The key hints to the buyer's learning style are the words she used: comfortable, laid back, homey.

Take 2

V: Hello, may I help you?

K: Yes, I am interested in lawn furniture that seats six to eight people. I really want something comfortable for my out-of-town guests coming in to visit this weekend.

V: Okay, something comfy that seats eight?

K: Yes, please.

V: Are you looking for anything in particular?

K: Yes, I want lounge chairs that you can sprawl out on.

V: We have a really comfortable lounging set with nice, thick cushions. It comes in a variety of cozy colors, and we can deliver within 24 hours.

K: Sounds interesting.

V: Let me show you. This way, please. Here you go. Give it a try and let me know how it feels to you.

K: Ooh! I could just fall asleep in these chairs. They're perfect! How much?

V: The entire set, including shipping, is $575. Would you like to put them on your charge?

K: No, thank you. I'll pay cash.

These are overly simple scenarios, but the second salesperson succeeded where the first one failed by listening to the customer and adjusting his own visually dominant style to mirror the customer's kinesthetic language.

Now, let's change it up a bit. Say this time a couple walks in. One is auditory and the other kinesthetic. Again, the salesperson is a visual learner (V), the husband is auditory (A), and the wife is kinesthetic (K). Fast forward to where the wife has already selected furniture she wants, and the husband chimes in.

Take 3

V: Hello, may I help you?

K: Yes, how much is this comfy patio set? If I don't get out of this lounge chair soon I'm afraid you'll have to come wake me up at closing time.

A: Now, hold on there, honey. First, could you tell me how we would maintain this material, and what kind of warranty it comes with?

V: Absolutely. First, ma'am, to answer your question, this set sells for $535. And you can sit in it all you want, although I have to say you'll find it even more comfortable at home. And sir, this fabric is a low-maintenance antimicrobial polymer with a patented weatherproof coating designed to resist stains, tears, or discoloration. A little soap and water on a rag to take the dust off is about all you'd ever need to do to it. It comes with a five-year warranty against tears, stains, or discoloration, and we can upgrade that to a lifetime guarantee for an additional $100, if you'd like. (Pause.) Does that answer your questions? Is there anything else you would like to ask me?

> **WORKIN' IT**
>
> When working with a group of customers, engage each of them in the conversation. Answer all of their questions; identify each one's dominate communication style, and mirror it back to each one individually. Don't leave anyone out.

Here's the close:

V: Thank you so much; I know you both will enjoy your new lawn furniture. I will have it delivered tomorrow, so that you'll have it before this weekend, when your company arrives. I know your company will feel at home when they sink into those cushy chairs, and by the way, here is the warranty agreement. Let me get you some free cleaning products for the furniture, and instructions on how to maintain it. You can take those with you now. Here is my card. If you have any questions, just give me a shout; feel free to call me anytime.

Reading Key Phrases

Here are some phrases that visual, auditory, and kinesthetic learners and communicators will use in their conversations. The key is to identify the types of phrases someone uses. These are clues to how they see, hear, or feel the world. To become a persuasive communicator, speak back the phrases they use.

Visual:

- I see what you're saying.
- Picture this.
- I need to see it to believe it.
- See, I told you so.
- Let me illustrate this for you.
- Focus on this.

Auditory:

- I heard what you said.
- Could you repeat that again, please?
- I told you that.
- Did you hear me?
- That resonates with me.
- I will repeat it one more time.
- Listen to me.

Kinesthetic:

- I understand.
- I feel the same way.
- I get it.
- That feels just about right.
- Let's keep in touch.
- We have a connection.
- That really hurt my feelings.
- I feel so bad.

Listen to someone's choice of words, and this will give you the inside scoop on how others communicate. By "reading" words, and then communicating back in the same language to the receiver, you will build rapport, connect with more people, and make more sales (or whatever your goals are).

Why does this work? Because mirroring allows the person you are communicating with to see themselves "reflected" in you. This creates the perception that you understand their needs, hear what they're saying, and see it from their point of view. It's magical, and simple to learn.

Here's another example:

> Message sender: "I am in the market to buy a new car. I've been driving this dumpy old can for a while, and it's getting me down. My kids are grown and out of college. Now it's my turn; I need a pick-me-up and a new image. I am also single and wanting to get out and start dating. I can't take someone out in this old puddle jumper! I'm looking for a babe magnet, something red and sporty. What can you show me?"

After reading this mini script, count how many words are visual, auditory, and kinesthetic. After you count them, determine whether this customer's dominant learning and communication style is visual, auditory, or kinesthetic, as well as their secondary style.

The answer is that visual is dominant, and kinesthetic is secondary. Given this knowledge, here's a spot-on response:

> Receiver's response: "I understand; your kids are grown, and you need a new boost. Let me show you a car that the ladies go crazy over! I can totally see you in this car; it will definitely give you the status you're looking for. It's our new sports edition. It comes in candy apple red or black obsidian. Do you what to see it and take it for a test drive to see how it feels?"

WORKIN' IT

When speaking to a large audience, remember that a group of any size is likely to include all three types of learners and communicators. Given that 6 of every 10 people are visually dominant, strong visuals are essential. To reach your whole audience, however, you must remember that the remaining 40 percent will be almost evenly divided between auditory and kinesthetic learners, and structure your presentation accordingly, incorporating interesting sounds and exercises.

Effective Communication

When communicating with a visual receiver, use words that paint a descriptive image in the mind of the receiver. For example: If you are talking about surfing, you might describe the emerald curls stacked 8 to 10 feet high, smooth as glass, glossy, with white frothy teeth nipping at your heels as you carved, writing your name across the face, claiming it.

When communicating with an auditory receiver, speak clearly and articulately, avoiding slang or words you cannot pronounce correctly. Use punctuation, pauses, and inflection when speaking.

When communicating with a kinesthetic receiver, speak more slowly, and use storytelling and personal experiences to connect. In sales, they often teach the "feel, felt, found" method of overcoming client objections as in: "I understand how you feel. Others have felt the same way. But I have found …"

Reading others' communication and learning styles provides clues to how others experience the world. Having the ability to read how others speak is a powerful, persuasive tool to connect with anyone, in any situation, by using their own language to connect.

The Least You Need to Know

- People learn and communicate through words (auditory), pictures (visual), and touch (kinesthetic).
- Sixty one percent of the general public are visual communicators and learners.
- Effective communicators mirror the style of the person with whom they are interacting.
- When addressing a large audience, use all three styles to reach everyone.

Body Talk

In this part, we'll take a trip around the world and explore what gestures mean in different countries—and which ones you'd be better off leaving at home.

Then we'll travel around the human body and discuss how body language is conveyed using different body parts. We'll learn what our eyes tell others—and if there is any such thing as "lying eyes." We'll explore how our hands work to convey meanings, what gestures are universal to human beings, and how our feet telegraph our feelings, too. We'll also explore how we can actually change our emotions through changing our posture and our facial expressions.

See What You've Been Missing

In This Chapter

- Reading eye movements
- Neuro-Linguistic Programming (NLP)
- Separating and storing memories via sensory and representational systems
- The truth about deception detection

You may have heard that eyes are the windows to the soul. You've already learned that eyes can talk. But are they really windows? And if so, are our deepest thoughts vulnerable to any Peeping Tom who wants to look in? Is it possible to draw the drapes, or is it even necessary?

In this chapter, we explore the myths and truths of eye movement—what they say, and what they don't. We explain Neuro-Linguistic Programming, or NLP, what it means, and what people *think* it means. And we give you a chance to read a few eyes yourself. When we're finished, you'll never look at eyes quite the same way again.

Eye Witness

What's the first thing parents say to children to make sure they're telling the truth? They say something like, "Look me in the eye and tell me you didn't ...." Only the most brazen child could bluff!

We all have experienced that guilty "sheepish" look, firsthand. It is hard for us to imagine others being able to lie without giving it away somehow. And so, law officers, judges, psychologists, human resource directors, educators, and corporate executives invest in truth-detection training, seeking the power of the "all-seeing" eye.

So is it always possible to tell when someone's lying? Do the eyes give you away? Let's look a little deeper.

NLP

Neuro-Linguistic Programming (*NLP*) began as a thesis project at the University of California, Santa Cruz, by Dr. Richard Bandler and Professor John Grinder. The duo's mission was to develop human behavior models to better understand why some people naturally excelled in certain tasks while others struggled or failed at the same tasks. Although largely discredited for its original purpose, this research did help clarify what the eyes do and don't reveal.

SAY WHAT?

Neuro-Linguistic Programming (NLP) is a controversial approach to communication, personal development, and psychotherapy developed in the 1970s that attempted to reprogram negative thoughts and behaviors by overlaying the observed language and habits of so-called "successful" people.

One of the more valuable aspects of NLP research was the identification of eye-accessing cues. Studies have found that the human brain imprints images in visual, auditory, and kinesthetic form from our experiences. These images are stored in our memory and are available for recall at a later time.

You may have noticed, in conversation, that people's eyes are not stationary. They tend to move from side to side and up or down during the conversation. This is the visual equivalent of the sound your computer makes when it is searching the hard drive for information.

NLP suggests that there is a strong correlation between different types of eye movement and the ways different people process information.

For example, if you ask a boy, "What color is your front door?" you may see his eyes move upward (and to the left or right, depending upon whether he is right- or left-handed). NLP suggests this means he is accessing and recalling information from the visual part of his brain. If he were to look down in response to this question, he may be recalling the information from some "felt," or kinesthetic experience.

YA DON'T SAY

Have you ever had anybody stare at you with that blank, "deer in the headlights" look? That blank stare is the eye-accessing equivalent of "Does not compute." This is a sign that you may be talking to someone in a way that is inconsistent with their learning and communication style. Such miscues occur when one party to a conversation is unable to see things from the other's perspective. ("I may hear what you're saying, but I just don't see it that way.")

Sensory or Representation Systems

From NLP, we now know that certain eye movements are physical manifestations of thought processes. By observing these movements, or eye-accessing cues, we can get a sense of how someone processes input and recalls stored information. These so-called sensory or representation systems are tied to the learning and communication styles discussed in Chapter 5.

Sensory or representation systems are how we separate and store our memories. For example, when you think about your grandmother, you might either look up to access your visual databank, or down to recall the kinesthetic scent of her fresh-baked apple pie.

Reading these cues can reveal how a person processes information: visually (seeing), auditorially (hearing), kinesthetically (feeling and emotion), or through auditory digital (internal reflection based on facts, figures, and logic, independent of external sensory input).

Look Here

Following are photos of the six most common directions that eyes may travel when someone is asked a specific question. Keep in mind, the patterns switch left or right depending on whether the subject is right- or left-handed.

Visual, recalled.

Visual, constructed.

Auditory, recalled.   *Auditory, constructed.*

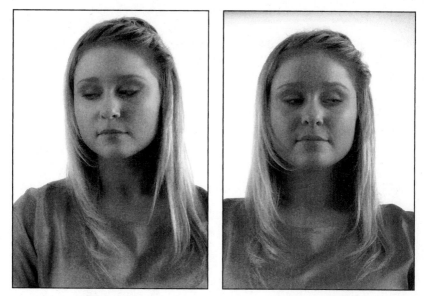

Kinesthetic.   *Auditory, digital.*

Eyes on the Prize

Now, put yourself in the place of the model in the preceding pictures. Try each of the following eye movements on for size. Assume you're right-handed. Don't move your head, just your eyes:

- Visual, recalled: Look up and to the left.

- Visual, constructed: Look up and to the right.

- Auditory, recalled: Look toward left ear.

- Auditory, constructed: Look toward right ear.

- Kinesthetic: Look down and to the right.

- Auditory, digital: Look down and to the left.

Now, flip the script and pretend you are left-handed. Swap left for right in the previous instructions; up and down remain the same.

However, like snowflakes, no two people are alike (thank goodness). Not everyone fits into one specific right-handed or left-handed system; we're just talking about tendencies. Suffice it to say that people's eyes often reveal their dominant communication and learning style. Variances between left- and right-handed people are less predictable.

WORKIN' IT

Can't remember where you left your keys? If you're right-handed, try looking up and to the left. If you're left-handed, look up and to the right. You just might get a visual picture of where you left them last.

No Eye Movement

If, when asked a question, the other person's eyes do not move anywhere, and they answer without delay and spontaneously, this indicates that the experience or event is close by.

The experience was not coded and stored in the memory, because the experience was so close, and thereby it is easily retrievable.

What's Your Style?

To determine your primary sensory or representational systems, ask yourself questions that require you to process in visual, auditory, kinesthetic, or auditory digital mode. See if you can find a fairly consistent pattern, then match the sensory or representational system that provides the closest match.

You can start with the following questions, but you'll probably get a better result by crafting questions that relate to your specific business or relationships. Practice on others as well. Track their eye movements and match them with the primary representational system:

- What was the color of your first car?
- What will your hair look like in 10 years?
- What does the sun feel like on your face?
- What did it feel like when you lost your first pet?
- When you sing to yourself, what do you sound like?
- What did your child's first words sound like?
- What three things would you add to your bucket list?
- How would it feel to swim in a bath of spaghetti?

Did you notice a pattern to your eye movements? What about others?

Building Your Eye Reading Skills

Knowing how someone thinks isn't the same as being able to read minds, but it can sure come in handy. It's a bit like dancing, though. You'll want to hone your skills in private, or in noncritical situations, where the stakes aren't very high. You'll be fine as long as you keep it simple and remember the basics.

People who process information visually tend to look up and visualize what they're thinking about. People who "think" with their ears look side to side. And people who "think" with their hands and feelings tend to look down.

Get in the habit of framing questions to match what you observe in the eye movements of others. Take note of their reactions, and keep practicing until it becomes almost second nature. Here are some scenarios to help you visualize the principles we've discussed.

The Big Chill

During a media training session on impromptu interviews, Kathleen broke character and stepped out of the mock studio.

"I just don't know if I can do this," she said, eyes drifting up and to the right.

It happened, literally in the blink of an eye, but Brad, a trained observer of body language, caught it. "Take me to where you are right now," he said. "What are you remembering?"

Kathleen responded, her voice small and tight, yet somehow relieved to be getting her secret out in the open. She bared her soul, sharing her great fear of freezing up on camera and embarrassing herself, like her best friend had done.

With the problem out in the open, Brad shuffled the agenda and spent the rest of the session in exercises that targeted Kathleen's fears.

Total Recall

Sonya was on a roll. Her sensible heels clicked smartly on the travertine tiles as she stalked the boardroom, waxing eloquent about brand essence, spin-offs, and the psychic benefit of having a beloved, if not dorky, mascot. She blasted through her vision of a vehicle for this mascot—a long, green, curvilinear convertible that would tour the country promoting the brand.

Her client, Irmagarde Gherkin, the pickle queen of Long Island, seemed to have tuned out. Her eyes were turned up and off to the left. Sonya could tell she was struggling to conjure a reasonable facsimile of this strange ride.

"Think Wienermobile, as a convertible pickle," she said, hoping that the recalled image would be strong enough to close the deal for her.

Irmagarde smiled. "We'll call it the Dill-orean."

Mixed Blessing

Jerry Mander, Regional Vice President of Hi-Lo for Spot-On Carpet, had put it off as long as he could. Pushing away from the dinner table, he cleared his throat and asked for his family's undivided attention.

"I've been offered a position in Berber," he said, puffing up his chest a little. "It's a big jump in pay, so little Jerry wouldn't have to sleep in the laundry hamper any more, but there's a catch. The job is upstate. We'll have to move again in three months."

Mrs. Mander, Sally to her friends, raised a hand to cover her mouth. Her eyes dropped down and to the right, as she thought about being uprooted again.

Jerry saw the look in Sally's eyes. The same look was reflected on the faces on all of his kids. They'd gone out of their way to make friends in the short time they'd been in town and he wasn't about to take that from them.

"Okay, okay," he said. "We'll put it to a vote. I'll abide by the family's decision."

Risky Business

Redd Herring, a financial advisor with Gaussian Copula Securities, let his eyes drift to the clock on the wall over his client's head. The client, Betty Tall, hadn't moved in more than a minute, not since he'd suggested that maybe she might want to take some of her money out of pay telephone futures and maybe invest it in some more conservative index funds.

As soon as he said it, she was gone. Her eyes rolled down and to the left. He could see her lips moving, but she wasn't saying anything—at least not that he could hear.

Redd waited. It couldn't have been more than two minutes, but it felt like an hour. Betty had been his client for years. And if there was one thing he'd learned in all that time, it was to let her take the time she needed to think things through.

He was just starting to reach his limit (time always travels slower through silence) when Betty finally looked up at him and asked a couple of follow-up questions. He answered, and she submerged again into her thoughts.

Another minute passed before she sat up straight and tapped her lacquered nails on his aircraft carrier of a desk. "Where do I sign?"

Lyin' Eyes

Yes, eyes are windows, but, as we've discussed, they are opaque windows that reveal thought processes, not the thoughts themselves. There is no certain way to tell what people are thinking, or whether they are lying, simply by looking in their eyes.

BODY BLOCK

There is no proven scientific evidence that looking down and to the left, or any other direction, means that someone is lying. In fact, there is overwhelming research to the contrary.

The Least You Need to Know

- Eye movements reveal thought processes.
- When reading eye movements, look for patterns.
- Learning to read eye movements can help improve communication.
- Eye movements do not reveal deception.

Cultural Gestures

Hand gestures have different meanings in different parts of the world—a fact some pop stars, and even heads of state, learned the hard way. By getting a handle on your hand gestures, you'll not only make a better impression, you may even avoid getting arrested or causing an international incident! Even if you never leave your hometown, it is important to realize how powerful and communicative gestures can be. You'd hate to send the wrong message.

In this chapter, we place hand gestures in their cultural context, provide a little background on various countries and their customs, and then offer a list of gestures to avoid. This chapter will be helpful when you're traveling or encountering people from other cultures when you're at the store, at your kid's baseball game, at the office, or anywhere. Some of it is pretty funny, and it will make you sound wicked smart at parties.

Illustrators and Emblems

Hand gestures typically fall into one of two categories: illustrators or emblems. Illustrators fill blanks or add emphasis, much like in those old silent movies, where gestures brought the story to life.

If you were to ask a guy on the street for directions, he would probably use hand gestures, instead of street names, to "illustrate" his points and guide you in the right direction. We cover illustrators in more detail in the next chapter.

Emblems, on the other hand, tend to be less helpful and more declarative, or "emblematic," conveying a complete thought or emotion. Giving a high five would be a good example.

Emblems are also cultural. For example the two-fingered "V" gesture with the palm facing out, known throughout America as a peace sign, means "V" for victory in the United Kingdom—thanks to Winston Churchill. It's a tricky thing, that "V." Palm out it's peace or victory; but palm in, well, let's just say you should be prepared to defend yourself.

YA DON'T SAY

Former President George H. W. Bush got a crash course in hand gestures during a visit to the Australian capital of Canberra, in 1992, when he flashed a "V" to the crowd as his motorcade passed through. In Australia, the "V" stands for victory, and he was on a victory lap after driving Iraq out of Kuwait in Operation Desert Storm. The problem was not the "V" itself, but the fact that he flashed it with the back of his hand facing the crowd—an obscene gesture akin to "flipping the bird."

He wasn't the first head of state to make that mistake. That honor goes to Winston Churchill, who is credited with creating the "V for victory" emblem—which has been slightly modified from its original form.

Who wouldn't like a hug and a pat on the back? The Queen of England, for one, as First Lady Michelle Obama learned—a split second after that knowledge would have saved her from an embarrassing gaffe.

The University of Texas produced a video to help an Italy-bound group of Longhorns avoid the likely fist fights that were sure to have followed a careless "Hook 'em Horns!" gesture—which in Italy means, "Your wife has been unfaithful."

Most travel agents and professional guides will give you a heads-up on emblematic hand gestures, if you ask, before you depart on any overseas trip. Here are a few common do's and don'ts to get you around the world and back, without landing in jail or losing your pearly whites.

Australia

As Americans, we know that Fosters is Australian for "beer"; the Outback is a casual dining chain based in Tampa; and the palm-in peace sign is a way for American heads of state to get face time on Australia's Funniest Home Videos. Almost everything else we know, we learned from Crocodile Dundee movies or The Crocodile Hunter.

Laid-back Australians don't stand on ceremony. They get along with most everyone. So on the theory that nothing—except maybe body language—goes without saying, here are some tips to make sure your trip Down Under is just bonzer.

Tip number one: Don't say bonzer. It's passé and condescending. And though Aussies may greet you and each other with a warm "G'day" or "G'day, mate," from you it would come across like a New Yorker trying to talk Texan.

In greeting, a polite handshake and smile are sufficient. Australians tend to be matter-of-fact, so keep your long-winded travelogues for other vacation destinations.

Gestures to avoid in Australia:

- The American peace sign is the victory sign in Australia, but a palm-in peace sign means, "go perform an unholy act on yourself."

- Thumbs up has only one connotation—roughly equivalent to the palm-in peace sign. They also use the middle finger and the European favorite of slapping the bicep and raising a fist. For such a laid-back group, they seem to have no shortage of ways to let you know where you stand.

- Stretching the hand out, palms up, curling fingers in and out, is the Aussie way of summoning a prostitute.

Belgium

Family is priority one in Belgium. Many have lived in the same area throughout their lives, sticking close to their roots.

Appearance matters; their homes, sidewalks, and front porch steps are spotless. God forbid you see any dirt on the floor. It's a disgrace to have tall, unkempt hedges and gardens in front of their houses.

Social etiquette is also very important. Dress well when going out. Image is second here only to family.

Introductions begin with a handshake—brief, light pressure. After you build rapport, a three-cheek air kiss, brushed lightly, alternating sides—never on the lips—says, "We're close friends."

This air kiss is an expression of friendship.

A handshake is also appropriate on departure.

Communication is logical and must be founded on good reasoning. Belgians love to engage in long-winded discussions. If you're late, you'll be judged unreliable.

Gestures to avoid in Belgium:

- Don't point your index finger or talk loudly, be overly casual, or have poor posture.

- Avoid kicking your feet up and feeling like you're at home.

- Never snap your fingers to get someone's attention—even a waiter.

- Avoid putting your hands in your pockets—you know you want to.

Cambodia

Cambodians don't respond well to aggressive, boastful communication styles. Interpersonal communication is based on humility and saving face.

For greetings, bow while bending forward with your hands held in prayerlike fashion. Cambodians have also adopted the western traditional handshake, but take your cues from the person you are interacting with—in other words, mirror.

It is polite to bring a small gift—fruit or candy—when invited to someone's home, and deliver it with both hands. When offered a gift, politely refuse at first, but always accept it, graciously, in the end, receiving it with both hands.

Punctuality is expected; meetings are not planned without an agenda and schedule. Relationships and mutual trust are important; keep negative comments to yourself.

Cambodians are up on nonverbal communication, so make sure you present a great first impression. Cambodians suppress showing anger, anxiousness, or irritation. A smile is more situational and can have many interpretations. For example, Cambodians may smile when they're feeling nervous or irritated, rather than when they're feeling happy. Also avoid long eye contact.

Gestures to avoid in Cambodia:

- Never touch a Cambodian on the head or anywhere above the shoulders, even a child.

- Do not use your left hand to touch, eat, or pass anything.

- Never point with your index finger—gesture with your right hand, palm up.

- When seated, never sit higher than the oldest person in the room.

China

Nonverbal communication speaks volumes in China. They pay close attention to facial expression, body language, and tone of voice. The Chinese mask their expressions by maintaining a neutral affect when speaking. It is improper to stare or make direct eye contact in crowded areas.

Pointing and beckoning is considered rude in China. Here's a handy gesture that will at least keep you from dehydrating while you figure out how to ask a waiter for the check: if you need a refill on your drink at a restaurant, just turn your cup upside down. This signals that it is empty and you need a refill.

Turning your cup upside down is the polite way to indicate you need a refill.

Gestures to avoid in China:

- The Fig (Got your nose!): Thumb between middle and forefinger. This is considered obscene.

- An upraised fist is also considered obscene.

- Don't point or beckon a person—this is reserved for dogs.

Chile

Being a coastal country convenient to the Straits of Magellan, Chile is a worldly country that has, over the years, been a popular emigration destination for most of Western Europe and Eastern Europeans seeking respite from oppressive regimes.

Home of the late Pulitzer Prize–winning poet Pablo Neruda, Chile boasts a 95 percent literacy rate and progressive politics, with women enjoying positions of power and respect. In fact, from 2006 to 2010, the President of Chile was a woman, Michelle Bachelet.

Chileans tend to be formal—with men standing when women enter, and greetings including academic and professional titles. A kiss on the right cheek among friends, in greeting, is common. When invited as a guest to a Chilean home, a hostess gift is expected. Manners matter.

Shake hands socially only when a handshake is offered; it is not expected. A firm handshake, direct eye contact, and a smile are expected in business.

Gestures to avoid in Chile:

- All of the typical European and American vulgar gestures are observed and understood.

- The concha: Palm up, thumb pressed to raised fingertips to form a shell—a reference to a part of the female anatomy—seems to be Chile's primary contribution to the world supply of vulgar gestures.

- Tapita: The okay sign, covered with the palm of the opposite hand, means essentially the same thing.

- Slapping your left palm against your right fist is considered vulgar.

- Holding both hands together in a fisted position is obscene.

- Lifting a fist upright at head level is also considered obscene.

- Palm of the hand up, with fingers spread, says "You're stupid."

The tapita is a vulgar gesture.

Raising a fist like this is considered obscene.

Slapping the left palm against your right fist is vulgar.

This gesture says, "You're stupid!"

East Africa

East Africans are group-oriented and community is important. They lend a hand and pull together. Upon greeting during a casual encounter, they shake hands shortly, and in more established relationships, the handshake is prolonged.

When female friends greet each other, they kiss each side of the cheek. In a male/female introduction, one may or may not shake hands. Speaking is often accompanied by gesturing.

- Various tribes greet each other by spitting at each other's feet.

- Friends shake hands with a quick slap of the palms followed by a light four-fingered grip.

The four-finger grip is a greeting between friends.

Gestures to avoid in East Africa:

- Pointing is considered rude.

- Beckoning with a crooked finger is also considered rude.

- Eating, greeting, writing, or really doing anything with your left hand is considered vulgar.

BODY BLOCK

In many cultures, especially in developing countries, greeting, eating, writing, or gesturing with the left hand is considered the height of disrespect. This originates both from the superstitious belief that the left hand is evil or "sinister," and the practical fact that, in the absence of toilet paper, people observed social customs with their right hand and personal cleansing with their left.

India

Indians have a hard time saying no in order to avoid disappointing you. Rather than telling you they are sold out of your favorite item, they opt to offer another option. This should not be taken as being dishonest; it's because they want to please you. They hope you can pick up on their nonverbal subtleties, because they dislike speaking about anything negative. They believe it is rude not to find something that pleases you. Shaking hands is customary; men shake hands with men, and women with women, but not women with men.

Gestures to avoid in India:

- Don't beckon with one finger, palm up.
- Cutis: Hook thumbnail on teeth and flick. It means what you think it means.
- Never touch the head of a person from India—the head is the home of the soul.
- Watch your step—pointing with your foot, or showing someone the bottom of your foot, is offensive.
- The "no left-handed gestures" rule applies. Sorry, left-handers.

Italy

Dress to impress, or you might as well stay home. Italians are fashion conscious and very particular about first impressions. Image projects one's status, education, and family background.

Greet Italians with a great handshake and direct eye contact, with a little enthusiasm, and you're in! If you've built a relationship with an Italian, greet them with an air kiss on both cheeks, starting on the left, then right. Men give an additional pat on the back.

Gestures are practically parts of speech in Italy. They have a gesture for everything. If a guy sees a pretty girl, for example, he may raise his right index finger to his cheek and twist it. This means "Hot stuff!" or literally "delicious."

This gesture means, "She's hot!"

Italians prefer close physical contact. It's common to see hugging between good male friends, and long handshakes with hands clasped hand over hand. Cheek kisses are common for both men and women.

The summoning gesture, for calling someone to come closer, is a scooping motion, with the palm down, as if drawing the person to you. To say good-bye, hold your hand, palm up, and clap your fingers repeatedly against your palm, like a grasping baby.

Saying hello and good-bye.

Italian gestures could fill a book by themselves. In the interest of time, here are a few gestures to avoid:

- Horns: The official hand gesture of the University of Texas Longhorns, in Italian, means that your partner has been unfaithful. The "I love you" gesture from American Sign Language also comes dangerously close.

- Index finger to the temple means "Are you crazy?"

- Hands thrown forward, palms up, is a gesture borrowed from Greece that essentially means "eat pig flop."

- All of the other European offensive gestures apply.

- Dragging the thumb from the right eye down the right cheek means "clever" or "wily," but is sometimes used sarcastically.

WORKIN' IT

The dismissive chin flick—portrayed in movies and television as an obscene gesture—is really just the Italian way of saying, "I couldn't care less."

Peru

Peruvians, like Italians, are notorious for using a lot of hand gestures to communicate. Because of their expressiveness, they tend to be quite animated. Peruvians speak softly, so avoid talking too loudly; it can be a real turn-off.

Peruvians are not the most prompt culture; they're more relaxed and less concerned about time schedules than Americans. Their focus is on family and relationships. Most Peruvian women are homemakers. Men prefer to do business with those they have known for a while, and with whom they have built trust over time; they require a strong bond before entering into any business relationship. Your rapport-building skills and first impressions will be crucial here.

Peruvians dress sharply when they go out, so keep those tourist clothes in your suitcase and break out your Sunday best. If you dress too casually, you'll be frowned upon.

Opposite sexes shake hands. When two men meet who know each other, they will shake hands and/or give each other a nice pat on the back. Women will often greet each other with a kiss on one cheek.

Peruvians stand close together when they talk, and maintain eye contact, almost to the point of staring. Be careful not to offend by standing too far away, and try to mirror their eye contact behavior.

The American okay gesture, turned upside down while verbally commenting "service was excellent," is considered a compliment—although, as a general rule, you might want to leave that gesture at home when you travel. Better safe than sorry.

The okay gesture turned upside down is usually considered polite.

If you see a Peruvian tapping their head slightly while you talk, this indicates, "I'm thinking."

Tapping the head shows the person is thinking about something.

The beckoning index finger is another gesture you may want to leave home in your sock drawer. In Peru, when you want someone to come closer, turn your palm toward the ground and use all of your fingers to draw them toward you.

Come here!

A Few More

Gestures have different meanings in different countries. If you don't know what you're doing, you could wind up with trouble on your hands. Here are a few more to keep in mind:

- Greece: Avoid the "stop" signal—the popular American "talk to the hand" gesture made famous by The Supremes; it's insulting. Also, the moutza gesture—both hands and fingers open and pushing away—is an offensive pantomime of throwing excrement.

The stop gesture is considered an insult.

- Pakistan: Never reach for food with your left hand; the left hand is seen as unclean. This is true of many other countries as well. It's probably best to fake being right-handed when you travel abroad.

YA DON'T SAY

Reading about all the different ways American gestures may offend people in other countries, you might be getting a complex. Let's flip the script. In some parts of Tibet, people will often stick out their tongue in greeting. It's an old custom dating back to the ninth century: The Tibetan king, Lang Darma, known for his cruelty, had a black tongue. As Buddhists, Tibetans believe in reincarnation, and they feared that this mean king would be reincarnated. Consequently, for centuries Tibetans have greeted one another by sticking out their tongues demonstrating that they do not have black tongues, that they are not guilty of evil deeds, that they are not incarnations of the malevolent king.

- Japan: Four fingers thrust in someone's face is the Japanese way of saying, "You're less than human; you're an animal."

Top Five Most Misunderstood Hand Gestures

The following gestures are innocent in some places and offensive in others. When in doubt, just keep your hands to yourself!

Circling your index finger at your temple:

- America, Germany: You're crazy.
- Argentina: You have a phone call.

Okay gesture:

- France: You're worth zero.
- Japan: Money.
- Brazil: A sexual orifice.
- Middle East: Sexual proposition.
- Peru, Brazil, Germany: Anus.

Thumbs-up gesture:

- America: Good job, all's well.

- Australia: Up yours.

- Germany: One, please.

Peace sign:

- America (palm out or in): Hippie solidarity, opposition to war.

- Great Britain, Australia, Ireland, and New Zealand: Palm out means victory; palm in means the same as flipping the bird.

And the queen mother of all misunderstood hand gestures ... Horns:

- America: Rock and roll; two outs; Hail Satan; or "I'm a Texas Longhorn fan."

- Italy: Your partner is cheating on you (horns down means blocks evil).

- Brazil and Venezuela: See Italy.

- Africa: Throwing a curse.

- Australia: Sign language for cattle; see Texas Longhorns.

- Russia: An insult aimed at the newly rich.

- Buddhism and Hinduism: Sacred hand, dispels evil.

- American Sign Language (horns, with thumb extended): I love you. Although this is actually based on the fact that the fingers in that position spell out ILU, it has been misinterpreted by some as satanic.

The Least You Need to Know

- Gestures may have different meanings in different countries.
- What may be perfectly acceptable in one culture may be offensive in another.
- To avoid inadvertent offense, brush up on the customs of another country before traveling there or attempting to communicate with people from there.

Illustrative Gestures

In This Chapter

- Communicating with your hands
- Putting gestures to work
- Using gestures more effectively

In the previous chapter you learned that gestures can have different meanings in different countries and that some cultures gesture more or less than others. In our recent world travels, we touched on how most gestures are either illustrators or emblems, but we dealt primarily with emblems. In this chapter we focus more heavily on illustrative gestures, exploring different styles, goals, and outcomes in everyday speech and professional communication. Although they all fall under the heading of "illustrators," you might rightly think of them as different paints on your easel—finger paints, although some illustrative gestures may bring your whole body into play.

Illustrating Your Point

Before we settle in to talk about gestures in a professional context, let's stretch our legs with another field trip and observe a few illustrative gestures in the wild.

Ah, Central Park—bicycles, balloons, and look, a mime! Talk about illustrative gestures. The guy's a walking silent movie. If he couldn't "talk" with his hands, he'd be just another quirky hipster with a white glove fetish. That clown over there—same story, he just has bigger shoes.

Have you ever played charades, or its more commercial cousin, Guesstures, where players act out a key word or phrase using body language? That's what illustrative gestures do, except that they enhance, rather than replace, the spoken word.

Let's explore some of the most common illustrative gestures and what they do.

Regulators

These conversational on/off switches govern verbal exchange. For example, you might raise a finger to indicate "I have something to say," or hold up a hand to discourage someone else from speaking. Regulating gestures are most often seen in two-way conversation—my turn and then your turn. You will sometimes see them used by masters of ceremony, pushing down with outstretched hands to quiet a crowd before introducing a speaker.

> **WORKIN' IT**
>
> A symphony conductor owes her entire living to regulatory gestures. Without a sound, she controls the actions of hundreds of musicians, with nothing more than a baton and an established pattern of gestures regulating tempo, volume, tone, timbre, and inflection.

Metaphors

A speaker trying to convey an abstract concept might give it shape and dimension with a gestural metaphor—such as interlocking fingers for teamwork; a sturdy, braced posture for grit; or a raised open palm for support.

Motivational speakers rely on this type of gesture to give substance and weight to philosophical and psychological abstractions.

Icons

First encountered in elementary school story time, iconic gestures tend to be the physical manifestations of easily recognized or "iconic" images: bunny ears, scissors, fists, and pantomime. Other examples include counting out talking points on your fingers or using an upward progression of horizontal chops to either represent vertical progress or increase importance. These are all iconic gestures.

Affectation

The intentional display of inner emotions, affect gestures might include someone jumping up and down and shaking their hands like maracas in excitement, covering their eyes or ears to block an unwanted sight or sound, crossing their arms, balling their fists, or holding their nose.

Unlike our early discussion on facial expressions, which tend to be unconscious, an affect gesture is an intentional signal, a pose or affectation, specifically selected to put others on notice.

Putting Gestures to Work

Now that you know *what* to do with your hands, it's time to apply it. Illustrative gestures are to speaking what performance is to music. Anyone can play a power chord on the guitar, but no one can windmill their arm and play without evoking the image of Pete Townshend of the rock band The Who. Illustrative gestures allow you to amplify your message and increase your power to persuade, motivate, and inspire. Here's how they do it.

Persuasion

Imagine a popular evangelist stalking the stage, dipping, swaying, preening, and playing to the crowd—loud, proud, and supremely confident. When you've got people counting on you to call down fire from heaven and banish the devil, you've got to bring your A-game.

Now substitute your favorite motivational speaker or charismatic CEO. See any similarities? Let's break it down:

- Do the speakers in your mind stand behind a podium, or do they move around the stage—setting their message in motion?

- Are they static or animated?

- Do they use the air space around them like a bulletin board, assigning certain ideas and concepts to different parts of the stage—with "good" thoughts both physically and metaphorically higher than "bad" thoughts, and problems separated, both physically and by tone of voice, from solutions?

- If they stand behind a podium, do they at least use hand gestures to arrange and display their thoughts in the air?

A persuasive speaker uses illustrative hand gestures to render thoughts into physical reality. The fact that the speaker can see them clearly enough to move them around in space and time makes them real. And getting people to see something is the first step toward persuading them to believe it.

 SAY WHAT?

In a scene from the movie *My Big Fat Greek Wedding,* about the power of persuasion, the mother tells her daughter how stubborn her father can be and offers a solution: "The man is the head. But the woman is the neck, and she can turn the head any way she wants."

She got that right!

Cooperation

President Barack Obama's favorite sport is basketball, a team sport that requires cooperation. The next time you hear him speak about cooperation, watch what he does with his hands. He holds them, chest-high, about a foot apart, palms facing in, like a point guard ready to pass the ball.

If you want cooperation from your staff, then when speaking, hold both hands with fingers open, spread apart, slightly rounded, as if you're gripping a basketball. Place the basketball grip outward toward your audience as in the following picture. Make sure you gesture with grace and poise, not hard and choppy.

A gesture of cooperation.

Motivation

Gestures that motivate are always presented in a moving, rhythmic fashion. This is the physical manifestation of saying, "Follow me!" Motivating others takes energy, and energy moves forward; therefore use gestures that move forward and outward. This is one reason so many motivational speakers eschew podiums. They move around the stage, like caged tigers, creating the impression that they are very excited about the message they have to share and creating the expectation that you should be just as excited after you've heard it.

Motivating gestures are forward and outward.

Inspiration

What do you think an inspirational gesture would look like? Remember what you've learned about consistency between words and actions being required for authenticity.

A good way to inspire people, in addition to evoking cooperation and motivation, is to appeal to their hearts. Open hands, palms up, with fingers open, say: "I'm open to share my experiences so that you can learn from them."

This is definitely one you'll see often in worship, but also among human resource professionals, self-help speakers, and mental-health professionals.

An open gesture, with hands up, expresses inspiration.

Compassion

Compassionate gestures are those that are held closest to the heart. Before the kick-off of the Super Bowl, the "Star-Spangled Banner" plays. The fans place their hand over their heart during the song; the same goes when we say *The Pledge of Allegiance*.

When communicating a heartfelt message, the words are often followed by a hand-to-heart gesture. When it is authentic, the audience will be moved to feel the compassion, so it can be a powerful, persuasive gesture.

A hand to the heart shows compassion.

Authority

To signal you have expertise in a subject, construct a mid-high steeple gesture. In court, you'll see experts testifying on a specific point making a steeple gesture. You will often see this used in contract negotiations and business meetings. Don't overuse or maintain the steeple gesture too long; otherwise it will come across as contrived and planned—like the greedy cartoon tycoon Mr. Burns on *The Simpsons*. Be sure to change it up a bit.

Donald Trump uses a knee steeple when seated, signifying extreme confidence. You'll often see Trump seated during interviews, leaning forward with elbows on knees and his hands steepled in between.

Visualization

Sometimes all it takes to win people over to your point of view is to get them to see it from your perspective. Time lines, bar charts, graphs, even statistical probabilities can all be effectively illustrated with visualizations or pictorial gestures.

Punctuation

Punctuating words with fingers, hands, and arms in a rhythmic motion grabs attention and emphasizes a point or meaning. These gestures can be used on each syllable or on anchor words. Short, one-beat gestures are best when making a point, and repeated rhythmic patterns drive your message home, if your goal is to be hard-hitting on a subject. Here are a couple of examples.

Short, one-beat gesture:

> "STOP (Punch hand), and LISTEN (Punch hand) to what is being said."

Repeated rhythmic patterns:

"Stop and listen to what is being said."

This quick motion with the finger emphasizes a point.

What Gestures Say About You

Most people wouldn't think of giving a speech without rehearsing it. Far fewer, however, think to rehearse their hand gestures—an interesting statistic when you recall that 61 percent of people process information visually.

Even the most carefully crafted speech can be sabotaged by poor performance. Let's go over some ways bosses have been known to go astray.

The Hammerhead

Unless you're holding a gavel in your hands in a court of law, the closed-fisted pound says, "Take a chill pill!" or "I mean it!" or "This is unacceptable!" Losing your temper almost always sends the wrong message, like, "It's my way or the highway." A more effective way to send an important message is with strong eye contact and a firm voice, punctuating your words on point.

The hammerhead can be seen as an expression of anger or frustration.

Blame Game

No one likes to be pointed at, including your kids, spouse, friends, or employees. So why do so many people point directly at someone? Jennifer Kunst, PhD, wrote in the October 18, 2011, issue of *Psychology Today* that pointing at someone else is your own projective identification, meaning we try to get rid of our own unwanted feelings by shaming others for our own shortcomings. Unless you are pointing someone in the right direction when giving driving instructions, or calling upon someone in a room who has a question, it's probably best to keep your pointer to yourself.

Directly pointing at someone is a way of blaming and shaming that person.

The Put Down

The hand press is seen with a palm facing toward the floor. Generally this gesture is used to quiet a room, or get someone to calm down. It is often perceived as patronizing.

The push press—palms away, pushing outward in a "whoa" motion— is a deflector or stopper. It is a gestural shove. No one likes to be pushed around.

The hand press can be a calming gesture, but it can also come across as patronizing.

Backward Wrist Slap

I call this one the pinball flipper flap. A poorly executed attempt at inclusion, this chest-high gesture may appear from the speaker's perspective to be a magnanimous opening of the gates of knowledge. From the audience's perspective, however, it looks like a backhanded slap, or a condescending "shoo" motion.

Dismissive and inadvertently rude, this one should be dug up at the roots and banished forever.

The wrist slap is a dismissive gesture.

The Limp Wrist

The opposite of the wrist slap, the limp wrist suggests ambivalence and insecurity. The very limpness and listlessness of it evokes the image of a dead fish—cold and clammy. Opt for more deliberate and persuasive gestures that will make you appear more confident.

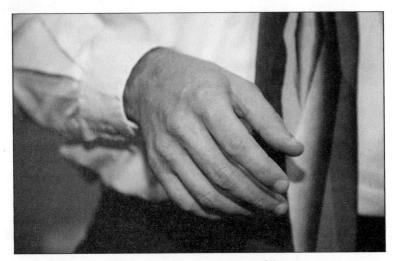

A limp wrist does not inspire confidence.

Do's and Don'ts of Gestures

Gestures can make or break you; they are an important piece of the body language puzzle. Keep these do's and don'ts in mind.

Do:

- Use gestures to make a point with spoken words.

- Use repeat-pattern gestures to drive your message home.

- Use "palms up" gestures to appear more truthful and "palms in" gestures to appear more inclusive.

- Use motion to motivate.

Don't:

- Point directly at anyone.

- Make "chopping" hand gestures.

- Hammer your point with your fists.

The Least You Need to Know

- There are several ways to illustrate a point using gestures.
- Gestures can be used in persuasive communication.
- Gestures can replace spoken words.
- Practice hand gestures before making a speech.

Display of Emotions

In This Chapter

- How to determine the authenticity of emotions
- How to understand your image
- How different emotions look

Emotions cannot hide. The body displays them in one way or another. This chapter shows you how that's true and what several different emotions look like and the common characteristics of each.

Central Casting

Let's say you're an actor and you're auditioning for a part in a new television show. You've been given a script and a character description. Now it's up to you to convince the casting director to pick you over all the other actors auditioning for the same part. To get the part, you have to be believable. You have to be authentic. To pull this off, you're going to have to draw on your emotional memory bank, and summon real feelings from your life that are similar to the ones described in the script.

Have you ever cringed through an actor's painfully inept performance in a community theater production, or found yourself completely captivated by an Academy Award–winning performance?

A skilled actor must convincingly portray a believable character and move an audience to feel as if the events they portray are real—or at least real enough to suspend disbelief.

> **WORKIN' IT**
>
> To pull off a character, actors rely on stored memories of past events to evoke the correct emotion for a part. Teachers, speakers, executives, and leaders of all types must draw on similar gifts to project confidence and competence amid the uncertainties of everyday life.

What's My Motivation?

Body language opens up a new channel of communication to an audience, to colleagues, and even to a partner or spouse. By becoming a student of how feelings look on the outside, you will gain a better understanding of the image you present to others and become better at detecting a variety of emotions, such as anger, suspicion, attraction, disdain, fear, and insecurity, when it's aimed at you.

> **SAY WHAT?**
>
> Anyone can create any emotion at any moment. All emotions are created. They don't come at you from outside. You decide to fall in love. You decide that a thing is funny, or sad. No one makes you angry, or makes you cry. No one makes you happy. That's all you, and if you're honest and sane, you know this is so.
>
> —Steven Horwich, Emmy Award–winning director, writer, and acting coach

Throughout the next few pages, you'll be presented with several body language photos. Look at the photos carefully, taking specific note of each feature: the eyes, forehead, mouth, legs, feet, shoulders, arms, fingers, hands, and head. How different body parts are displayed and carried by someone is the formula to their feelings and emotions.

Confidence

When a confident person enters a room, you know it. Heads turn in acknowledgment. But why is that, exactly? It begins with a high level of self-esteem. People gravitate to positive energy and those who exude it. It looks like this:

- Squared shoulders
- Uncrossed legs, arms, and hands
- Open body language
- Body parallel with another's
- Direct eye contact
- Takes up space
- Stands with legs shoulder-width apart
- Walks with purpose

Physical signs of confidence.

Low Self-Esteem

No one wants to place their confidence in people who don't have confidence in themselves. Low self-esteem is almost impossible to mask. It leaks out in some of the following ways.

- Closed or cringing posture
- Arms crossed below the waist
- Poor eye contact; often looks down or away
- Takes up little space
- Rounded shoulders
- Takes short, tentative steps, and may even drag feet
- Awkward or unnatural gestures
- Candlestick legs—legs closed and together, or crossed at ankles.

Physical signs of low self-esteem.

Arrogance

Arrogance is not confidence. Confident people feel competent from the inside out; they have strong opinions and know who they are. An arrogant person is the emotional equivalent of putting perfume on a skunk—false bravado over an insecure core. By looking down on others, they elevate themselves with the following gestures:

- Hands behind head
- Distance—positioned farthest away
- Nose tilted slightly up, or protruding chin
- Crossed arms
- Smirk
- Puffed-up chest

Physical signs of arrogance.

Deception

As we said at the outset, there's no one sure way tell if a person is lying, but liars do leave some clues. Look for the following:

- Body that angles away from others when talking
- Fidgety hand to face and neck gestures
- Excessive eye contact
- Rapid blinking
- Crossed arms and/or legs

Physical signs of deception.

Flirtation

Just like a peacock fluffing its feathers, humans use preening gestures to prepare for courtship. Intimacy requires close space, but flirtation can occur from across the room.

The infamous hair toss, coy head tilt, leg display, and heel slipping slyly out of a dangling sling-back shoe are all signals of flirtation for women. For men, grooming gestures, like adjusting the shirt cuffs, combing their hair with their fingers, the burly bouncer stance with arms crossed and wide stance say, "Hello ladies!" A few others for both sexes are:

- Dilated pupils

- Close body contact

- Flushed skin

- Chest protrusion

- Hands in pockets, thumbs out

Physical signs of flirtation.

Anger

From mild frustration to insensate rage, some of these volcanic gestures have been known to spark 911 calls. Most of us have seen enough of these:

- Clenched fist
- Furrowed brows
- Lips pulled tight and stretched horizontally
- Hard walk
- Clinched and/or pulsating jaw muscles
- Piercing eye contact

Physical signs of anger.

Nervousness/Anxiety

Nervousness is often accompanied by anxiety. To an observer, an anxious person appears uneasy in their surroundings and sometimes in their own skin. Emotional leakage surfacing as nervous energy looks like this:

- Fidgetiness
- Rapid eye-blinking
- Cracking voice
- Excessive thirst
- Grooming or self-soothing gestures
- Rapid breathing

Physical signs of nervousness or anxiety.

Depression

With symptoms ranging from mild to chronic, a depressed person looks as if the energy has been sucked right out of them. Movements are slow and sluggish, punctuated with deep sighs and erratic breathing. Self-pity is often expressed through sad expressions and a pouting chin. Depression is often accompanied by guilt, shame, and despair, following a disappointment or loss. Characteristics of depression are:

- Slouching
- Eyes downcast
- Head hanging
- Eyes unfocused, or closed for long periods
- Hand-wringing
- Rubbing face or neck

- Furrowed brows, pulled together with horizontal lines across forehead
- Protruding lower lip and/ or raised chin pout
- Slumped shoulders
- Lifeless arms
- Empty or absent appearance

Physical signs of depression.

Self-Doubt

A self-doubter's verbal communication is often rife with long pauses, suggesting that they're never quite sure of what they are saying. This person's words and actions are often out of sync as they try to appear more confident than they are, but underlines every action with a micro-expression of underlying doubt—biting their lip, or lifting their eyebrows in an almost frightened expression. Look for the following:

- Bottom lip bite

- Eyes asking a question, rather than giving an answer

- Double shoulder shrug that means, "I don't know"

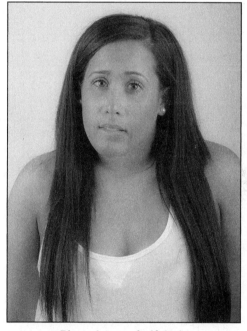

Physical signs of self-doubt.

Listen to Me!

"Stop and pay attention," this person is saying nonverbally, "I have something to say." They might point their index finger right at you, as if to say, "Yes, you; that's who I'm talking to." Or out of desperation to get you to listen, you may see exasperation in their facial expressions or hear it in their voice, raised to a high pitch, along with some of the following body language:

- Close distance
- Hands and arms extended
- Palms stretched open, fingers apart
- Leaning at the waist, extending out from the torso
- Pointing the index finger
- Rapid slicing or chopping hand gestures
- Eyebrows raised, eyes wide open and fixed in place

This bossy employer leaves the employee feeling anxious, insecure, and ashamed.

Critical

There's a skeptic in every crowd. Look for some of these telltale signs:

- One eyebrow raised
- Concealed smile with lips together, stretched horizontally
- Laughing or giggling
- Both hands clenched together with one pinky pointed upward
- Peering above their glasses
- Pointing an index finger at another person

Physical signs of a skeptic.

Power Play

There's nothing pleasant about this duel for dominance. The power play is often seen in couples, mediations, and business conflicts. The displays of power are seen in both group communications and one-on-one. This shows a stand-your-ground attitude with only one agenda: "Mine"—a win/lose proposition. Look for the following:

- In-your-face intimidation

- Hand behind the head

- One or both eyebrows raised

- Leaning into your space, and then leaning back farther away (may be accompanied by a smirk)

- Dominating the conversation

- Chopping or "hammerhead" hand and arm gestures

- Eyes averted, and appearing disinterested when another person is speaking

Physical signs of a power play.

Appreciation

Appreciation is sincere gratitude. Saying, "Thank you so very much for all you've done. I just want you to know how much I appreciate your kindness and support." Here's how it looks with the audio off:

- Hand over hand gesture

- Warm smile

- May appear emotional

- A handshake accompanied by a hand-to-shoulder grip

- Close distance

- A hug

Physical signs of appreciation.

Crossed Arms: The All-Purpose Gesture

Crossed arms are often perceived as signs of having a negative reaction, but a group of guys huddled in the hall at work may all have their arms crossed and be mirroring each other, which is a rapport-building gesture that shows everyone is doing the same thing and is on board.

Of all the gestures you may observe, crossed arms may have the broadest range of meanings. Here is what some of the most common meanings look like:

Cold.   *Bored.*

Defiant.

Guarded.

Insecure.

Dominant.

Thinking.   *Comfortable.*

The Least You Need to Know

- Emotions and feelings are clearly displayed in body language, whether you want them to be or not.
- Confident people display open body language, make appropriate eye contact, and walk with a sense of purpose.
- Before others can believe an emotion you feel, you have to believe you are feeling it yourself.

Best Foot Forward

In This Chapter

- What someone's feet are telling you
- How to read feet
- Which scenarios to learn by

Just like other body parts we've talked about, feet are conduits of someone's emotions as well. It may be hard to believe, but after you know what to look for, you'll be reading someone like a book just by looking at what they're doing with their feet.

In this chapter, you learn how emotions leak through our feet and give us away, even when we're wearing shoes. You also learn to read the subtle clues that reveal when someone is interested in you or is telling you to put an egg in your shoe and beat it; if they don't have time to talk; or whether you're invited to join in the group discussion or are being shunned. Here are some scenarios to show you how it works.

Exit, Stage Left

Ladies, have you ever been caught a tortilla shell short of a taco and had to run to the store in your grubbies, with no makeup or manicure? You dash down the ethnic foods aisle only to run into Diamond Jane Gotrocks, in her full-length mink, waiting for the stock boy to deliver her special-ordered steel-cut, hand-ground mustard.

You consider throwing it into reverse and waiting her out in the next aisle, or maybe reaching through to snag what you want without being discovered. But it's too late.

"Hey-ey" she says, waggling her diamond-dappled fingers and poodling over for an air kiss. "Dahlink. You've really let yourself go," she says.

You square your shoulders and break brave, trying to pull off an off-setting gossip block. "It's so good to see you, Jane. I didn't know you did your own shopping. What happened, did your pool boy move out?"

Jane's lips draw thin and tight. Your gambit is dangerously close to working, until her eyes are drawn down to your yellow Crocs, and she smiles a wicked crocodile smile of her own.

The direction your feet are pointing tells her the truth. You may be fronting brave with your squared shoulders, but your feet are screaming "Let's get out of here!"

All you can do at that point is grab your taco shells and take the walk of shame in your yellow rubber shoes to the checkout, hoping you don't run into anyone else you know.

Enter, Stage (F)right

Jennifer is attending her husband Brock's annual company awards banquet. She hasn't seen many of the employees since last year at the same event. Brock is a social butterfly, flitting around the room, checking in with all his work buddies. Jennifer, who is more of an introvert, is feeling a bit overwhelmed.

Brock stands face-to-face with a co-worker. Their feet are parallel—a sign of rapport. Jennifer is standing with her feet tightly together, sole to sole and heel to heel, like bowling pins side-by-side. What Brock fails to recognize is that Jennifer is feeling a bit insecure.

When the feet and legs are held closely together like candle sticks, this shows low confidence for an already shy, introverted Jennifer.

Jennifer's stance in this picture shows she's feeling left out.

What can Brock do to make Jennifer feel more secure, confident, and included? He can move his feet to form an open triangle that includes Jennifer and his co-worker. This would pull her into a three-way conversation, rather than continuing a one-on-one with the co-worker, excluding Jennifer. This helps encourage Jennifer to be an equal participant in the conversation.

This foot triangle allows Jennifer to feel included in the conversation.

Foot Rapport

Your company just landed a big marketing client. Congratulations! The table is all set up, and the seating arrangement has you next to the client. Your boss is giving the presentation at the front of the conference table, and you are seated between the client and the place your boss is standing. You notice that your client's left leg is crossed over his right, facing the presenter.

Being respectful to the presenter, it is always polite to face the person who is speaking, but you must also maintain rapport with your client. You can make the situation work by crossing your legs in the same direction as your client.

This seems like common sense to some, but you'd be surprised how many people would plant both feet firmly on the floor, and not follow the client's sitting position. Angling feet in the same direction subconsciously creates rapport and commonality.

Crossing your legs to mirror your client is a signal of rapport.

When seated, don't ever show the sole of your shoe. This occurs when you're seated and one foot is bent parallel to the floor, showing the worn sole of the shoe. In some cultures, that is considered offensive. Here in the United States, thin or holey soles suggest a lack of attention to detail.

Showing the sole of the shoe can also represent a feeling of inadequacy.

Rocking It

They say that many business deals are made out on the golf course, so you've planned an outing with a client for a round of golf, planning to relax and maybe drop a few hints along the way about a really cool business venture.

After your round, you retreat to the clubhouse for conversation over a drink or two. You begin to talk more in depth about the proposed venture, hoping to get your client's attention.

You notice your client is rocking up and down on his feet like a teeter-totter on the floor. This motion signals his interest and anticipation. Being the great foot reader you are, you can read that the client is very interested in the opportunity, just by his feet. This is your opportunity to seal the deal and get him on board.

Rocking on the feet can signal anticipation.

Tenuous and Solid Ground

Your boss calls you into his office to go over the sales numbers from last quarter. You know they're not good and your department did not meet its quota. You're flooded with the uncertainty of whether you'll have a job after the meeting. "What is the boss going to tell me? What will I tell my wife? What will she think?"

As you enter the office, he says, "Take a seat." You comply, folding your right leg to form a figure four over your left knee, and grabbing hold of your ankle to brace yourself for the news. Your foot is wiggling up and down.

Holding your leg can signal tension.

Good news! The boss didn't call you in to fire you. He just wanted to talk strategy. In fact, he compliments you and thanks you for all your hard work. You can feel your fear ebb.

As the meeting adjourns, you stand, feet firmly planted, shoulder-width apart, toes turned out slightly—a stance that says, "I'm on solid ground."

When interviewing for a job as a litigant, employer, leader, manager, or CEO, the on-solid-ground foot stance is perceived positively.

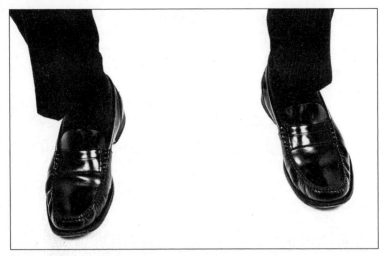

This stance indicates stability.

The Ankle Cross

The ankle cross has a few different interpretations. If the legs are extended and crossed at the ankles, it is seen as a relaxed state.

Legs crossed at the ankle is also a runway model stance.

The mood changes when legs are stretched out, crossed at the ankles, and the hands are held behind the head. This can signal dominance, arrogance, or control.

Legs that are crossed at the ankles and pulled in under the chair signal insecurity or feeling left out.

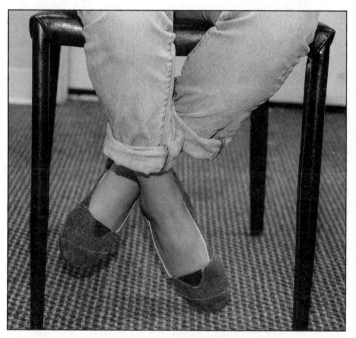

When you pull your crossed feet under a chair such as in this picture, you indicate you're feeling left out.

Foot Flirt

When a date is interested in you, you'll notice their feet and toes will align with yours. You'll see this when two people are seated in chairs side-by-side. Your date crosses their legs in your direction, while your legs are crossed inward, toward your date, as if your toes are almost touching or are turned in toward each other.

This mirroring shows interest in the other person.

If your date's feet and legs turn away from you, they're saying nonverbally "I'm not interested."

See ya!

Time to Go

If your date crosses their legs toward you, and at the same time points their toes in the opposite direction, they are telling you they are ready to call it a night.

> **YA DON'T SAY**
>
> What you see on the surface is not always what it seems. The feet are like a human compass—their direction is a clue to where the body wants to go.

Having the feet turned away shows the person is ready to leave.

Brace Yourself

You are about to take a ride on a roller coaster. You're strapped in and ready to take off. Before the ride begins, you grab the harness and hang on for dear life. Similarly, when your feet are wrapped around the legs of the chair, you're saying, "Brace yourself; we're in for a bumpy ride." This posture is often seen with people who are feeling left out or a bit insecure.

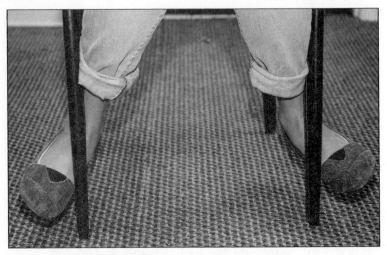

This bracing gesture indicates insecurity.

The Kick Back

Honey, did you get the popcorn? Ahh, yes! It's movie time. Stretch those legs out; it's been a long day and it's time to relax.

A relaxed gesture.

It's Time to Leave

The angles of the body, feet, and legs reveal where they want to go. It's much like driving a car; when you twist the steering wheel left, the car will go left; when you twist right, it goes right. Have you ever experienced driving home from work when your body is on auto pilot? You're almost home, and you realize, "I don't even remember how I got here." Reading the angles of the body, feet, and legs can tell you what direction you want to go, sometimes before you even actively walk out the door.

YA DON'T SAY

Did you know that when you are embarrassed the neck of your big toe blushes? British foot-reader Jane Sheehan, author of *Let's Read Our Feet,* does. Sheehan says she can tell a lot of things about people by the condition of their feet. For example, when someone is depressed, they tend to put more weight on the front of their feet, resulting in thicker, darker skin on the toe pads.

This is often seen in criminal investigations, also. When interviewing a suspect, the law enforcement officer looks for clues that the suspect is feeling on edge and might be ready to bolt.

Here's another clue that someone has a few tricks up their sleeve. You're at the airport, ready to walk though security. You remove your shoes, belt, and any electronic equipment you have in your briefcase. The security officer looks at you and notices that your body, legs, and feet are turned toward the exit, with only your head facing the officer. It may trigger the officer to look inside your bags to see what you might be hiding.

Dr. Paul Ekman, the researcher we talked about in Chapter 4 who identified all those facial expressions, also observed travelers at an airport. He found that people who angled their body, legs, or feet toward the exit often concealed items in their bags that were unable to pass through inspection, such as cigarettes and alcohol.

Of course, there are other reasons. They could be late for their flight, and might have been saving face by making eye contact, but their feet were pointed toward the terminal because they were in a hurry.

Floor Tap

You're at the poker table and have just been dealt a great hand of cards. Your legs begin to tap dance on the floor. The excitement goes right down to your toes, and your happy feet begin to applaud silently. If you really have a hard time containing your excitement, the back of your chair will begin to vibrate. If you really do play poker, you may want to train yourself out of this habit and begin to look for it in your opponents.

Unlike the excited foot tap which includes both feet, tapping one foot signals impatience.

Reading Feet for an Advantage

It's simpler to use reading feet to your advantage than you might think. Here are some more examples in everyday experiences:

- If you're passing a co-worker in the hallway and you stop him to get his attention, but you notice his feet are pointed straight ahead, just give him a pat on the back and say, "Hey, let's catch up later."

- If you notice your assistant's legs pulled in like a turtle hiding under a shell, you know that she is feeling a little insecure. So this would be a good time to give her some positive reassurance.

- When you see your date's toes pointing the opposite direction of his crossed legs, it's a signal that he's bored and ready to exit; end the date before he does. Or, if you don't want the date to end so soon, find a topic that interests him and use the mirroring techniques you learned in Chapter 1 to get him interested in staying a little longer.

- If you notice your sales prospect rocking back and forth on his feet, seal the deal right then.

The Least You Need to Know

- The direction of your feet indicates where you want to go.
- The feet reveal internal dialogue.
- Pay as much attention to feet as you do to the rest of the body when it comes to reading body language.

Deception Detection

Let's face it; one of the most valuable uses of body language reading is to determine if folks are being honest. But can you actually tell, on a reliable basis, when someone is lying?

We'll explore types of lies, look at why people (especially kids) lie, and determine some verbal clues that can help indicate deception. You'll also learn to use these tools with extreme caution, because there is no one foolproof test to reveal dishonesty.

Why Kids Lie

In This Chapter

- Motivations for lying
- White lies versus dangerous deceptions
- Signs your kid is being bullied

Kids and lying go together like peanut butter and jelly. It's part of being a kid. But it's important to understand and be able to detect the difference between small harmless fibs and big consequential deceptions. Kids are capable of both and everything in between—just like adults—for a variety of different reasons.

In this chapter, you learn why kids lie; the motives behind their lies; and how to spot lies. We discuss when to take a lie seriously and when not to overreact, how peer pressure affects our kids, and how your parenting style may contribute to your kid's lying.

Why Do Kids Lie?

Kids lie for all kinds of reasons. They may lie to seem smarter or dumber, depending on the audience. They may lie to seem richer, poorer, more athletic, or worldly. But there is one common thread to when kids lie: risk versus reward. Kids lie when the perceived reward for telling a lie exceeds the perceived risk of getting caught. For example, a child facing certain punishment over something may risk a lie for the possible reward of not getting punished. The greater the gap between the reward and the risk, the greater the motivation is to lie.

Motivation: The What Behind the Why

To understand why kids lie so often, let's understand why they lie at all. The answer varies with age. A preschooler may be unable to clearly distinguish between fantasy and reality. A kindergartner may lie to avoid punishment or to get a parent's attention. Preadolescent lies tend to fall into either of these categories, with the possible addition of work avoidance. It is usually not until a child hits their teen years that dangerous lies are encountered that will keep you up at night.

The motivations for kids to lie include:

- Fear of punishment
- Personal gain
- Peer pressure
- To protect themselves from harm
- To protect someone else from harm
- Fear of embarrassment or shame
- To gain admiration or attention

Fear of Punishment

Top on the list of motives for lying, for kids of all ages, is the fear of punishment—both real and perceived. Kids' fears can stream from unrealistic parental expectations and pressure, severe punishment or threats, excessive pressures, and mental and physical injury.

Clinical psychologists have found that kids who lie excessively tend to have poor self-esteem and should be treated with care and understanding, rather than punishment. That's not to say there should not be consequences for bad behavior, but rather that the punishment should fit the crime and be handled in a constructive way to help the child learn from the experience as opposed to worsening an already damaged self-esteem.

The signs of fear of punishment include:

- Body language angles away from parent
- Body language curls up and leans away, or curls into fetal position
- Shields face with hands and arms
- Eyes opened wide, showing whites above the pupils
- Grooming gestures—wringing of hands
- Nervousness and fidgeting
- Mouth stretched horizontally
- Dry mouth

Signs a child is in fear of punishment.

Here's a scenario demonstrating a lie based on fear of punishment: A teen sharing homes between two divorced parents lost, not her first, or second, but third dental retainer. Afraid that her father would yell at her, the teen concocted an elaborate tale to avoid punishment. She asked her mother to take the fall and pretend that the retainer melted during disinfection—a story that turned out to be not too far from the truth, when the retainer turned up melted in the clothes dryer. In this case, the fear of punishment prompted the teen to lie and make up a story, and therefore reap the reward of avoiding her father's wrath—either real or perceived.

Personal Gain

Kids also lie to get what they want. A student might cheat on a test to get a better grade. In this case, the reward of getting a good grade is perceived to be greater than the risk of getting caught.

When you were a kid, did you ever play one parent off of another, asking one for permission to do something and saying that the other parent said it was okay, even though that wasn't true? Did you ever lie and say that you finished your homework, even though you hadn't, in order to watch a favorite television show? Those are lies for personal gain. They aren't whoppers, but you get the drift.

Peer Pressure

Peer pressure is real and getting worse, thanks to electronic media. The pressure to be thin, to be more attractive, to drive a nice car, to wear designer jeans, and to sport a celebrity hairstyle makes many teens feel insecure.

Also, the pressure among teens in America to indulge in unsafe sex, drugs, and alcohol is epidemic. Teens are joining dating websites, posting scantily dressed photos of themselves, and indulging in R- and X-rated conversations, i.e., sexting. In 2010, the FBI estimated that 20 percent of teens transmitted naked pictures of themselves by phone or online; others place the percentage at closer to 30 percent. Either way, you get the idea.

The perceived reward, in this case, is acceptance. The desire to be liked and accepted is so strong for teens they will do anything to be so. Unfortunately, the risk of these behaviors is much greater than the teen mind is developmentally capable of processing. It can result in issues becoming embarrassingly public, reputations ruined, or worst of all, lives lost. Additionally, the cyber landscape is rife with predators who prey on isolated teens. Like wolves in sheep's clothing, they offer acceptance yet deliver degradation, guilt, captivity, and even death.

As you can imagine, particularly with regard to sexting and other teen explorations, peer (and pervert) pressure and related behaviors provide fertile ground for lies and half-truths.

Protect Themselves from Harm

In the case of bullying, kids have reported that they fear being picked on more or getting hurt by reporting it, so they opt to keep it to themselves or lie about the fact it is happening. Kids who have been physically or sexually abused often remain silent, because they fear that saying anything will only increase the abuse.

Bullying is an all-too-common problem for kids, so watch for the signs.

Abusers threaten and coerce their victims by constantly keeping them in fear. We saw this in the nationally reported Elizabeth Smart case, where the young girl was snatched from her own bedroom by a groundskeeper and held captive for months. She had many opportunities to escape, but didn't try, fearing for her life.

Signs that a child is being bullied or abused are the following:

- Diminishing self-esteem—listen for negative emotion such as hate, despise, disgusting, kill, I'm ugly, I'm stupid, etc.
- Demand for material items
- Unhappiness
- Irritability
- Cuts and bruises

Protect Others from Harm

Kids may lie to protect friends and family. For example, a daughter coerced by her mother into stealing toiletries takes the rap for it when caught to keep her mother from going to jail.

Children have also been known to lie, in cases of abuse by a family member, for fear of breaking up the family and upsetting others.

Fear of Embarrassment or Shame

It is common for kids to lie to avoid embarrassment or shame. For instance, a new teen driver, relegated to driving Dad's jalopy with the cracked windshield and a coat-hanger for a radio antenna, might park a few blocks from school to avoid having to defend his wretched ride to his classmates.

Upon running into a classmate unexpectedly, he might disown it, claiming it to be a loaner only, while his cooler car is in the shop.

Gain Admiration or Attention

"Mom and Dad, you won't believe what just happened!"

When you hear this from a kid, you're bound to be suspicious, and rightly so. It's a setup for a stage performance. The attention-seeker and storyteller likes to be the center of attention. They can't stand for anyone else to be in the spotlight and they'll go to great lengths to turn the conversation back to themselves, even if they have to make something up.

These gestures indicate a child is lying to gain attention.

Signs of lying to gain admiration and praise include:

- Stories that sound too outlandish to be true

- Use of exaggerated words and phrases

- Use of large hand and arm gestures

- Talking loudly

- Giving overly descriptive detail about irrelevant facts

- Leaning forward into your space

- Looking to see if others are watching

BODY BLOCK

Little white lies (the common house lie) can be the hardest to detect. The bigger the lie, the more nonverbal deception clues the liar leaves behind. When there is no fear of getting caught, it is difficult to tell whether you're being lied to.

White Lies

You've just bought some new make-up and model it for your 15-year-old daughter. You line up your purchases on the bathroom counter where they'll be ready for you to work your magic in the morning.

The next day, your new mascara is missing. You look high and low but it's nowhere to be found. That night, it's back on the counter, but much closer to the edge and nowhere near where you first left it. You ask your dimpled darling if she had seen your mascara. She gives you the big eyes and says: "I didn't touch it."

Guilty, with a slip of the tongue. You didn't ask if she had touched it. You asked if she had seen it. Taking your new mascara and trying to put it back without you knowing it isn't the end of the world. Does it deserve a grounding for a week? Probably not. In this type of situation, the culprit is more embarrassed than anything, and may just be afraid to ask or let you know she's out of mascara or would like to try yours.

Hands over the mouth are a sign a child is concealing or hiding something.

Here are more clues that your little angel may be hiding horns beneath a halo:

- Hands over mouth
- Conceals items behind their back or in their clothes
- Ditches items and dashes out of a room
- Unusually quiet
- Lays body over hidden object to conceal it
- Fidgety

If little white lies like the preceding examples go on all the time with your child, then you likely have a bigger issue on your hands to address, such as low self-esteem, communication problems, or a need for attention.

Trust, but Verify

We know that kids lie and we've examined the motives behind these lies. The question we must consider now is this: when should you, as a parent or responsible adult, do something about it, and when should you let it slide?

Sometimes parents and adults need to reexamine whether they are setting themselves up to be lied to. Being too harsh or having unrealistic demands and expectations of your children can drive kids to lie.

BODY BLOCK

Parents should avoid the "gotcha." Finding the truth is more important than detecting lies. Provide a safe place for your children to open up without the fear of punishment. Often, lying increases when there are problems in the home or something in the family dynamic has shifted.

It's a fine line. Kids are eager to please and they have a habit of telling adults what they think we want to hear. On the other hand, your kids may be withholding that they're being bullied or that they're having self-esteem issues. Keep a close watch and find time to talk to your kids—and don't believe every word they say. Trust, but verify, as President Ronald Reagan was fond of saying. Look for anything that appears different or off; often there is stuff going on that you may have no clue about.

The Kelly Conundrum

A teenager named Kelly doesn't come home at curfew. It's 10 o'clock on a school night. Kelly said she was going to the movies with her friend Lisa. Kelly's mom tries her cell phone and it goes straight to voicemail. She calls Lisa, who says, "I haven't seen her all day."

Kelly's mom calls every one of her daughter's friends that she has phone numbers for. No luck. She thinks about calling the hospitals but decides the police are a better option.

It's now 10:45, and as Kelly's mom stands in the kitchen, phone in hand, dialing 911, guess who saunters in? Emotionally exhausted, Kelly's mom struggles with whether to hug her daughter or throttle her. Through tears of anger and relief she manages: "Where were you?"

Kelly responds, "I told you, I was with Lisa. The movie got over late, and we stopped at McDonald's on the way home."

Anger surges ahead of relief for Kelly's mom: "Excuse me? I just spoke to Lisa, and she told me she hadn't seen you all day!"

Kelly's deer-in-the-headlights look says it all as she angles her body toward her bedroom door, in hope of escape from hearing the inevitable, "You're grounded!"

Kelly's eyes begin to flutter; her mouth becomes dry; she runs a hand through her hair; folds her arms; and bows her head in surrender. Busted.

Kelly was telling partial truths. She did go to the movies, but it was not with Lisa; it was with Brock, a young man she had been forbidden to see because of his misdemeanor conviction for marijuana possession. The movie got over at 9:00; they went to McDonald's and stopped at a friend's house.

Busted!

WORKIN' IT

According to Dr. Ekman, lying and concealing information are both lies. Lying is the deliberate approach to misleading you. Your kid knows the truth and intentionally misleads you to believe something other than the truth. Concealing is the deliberate hiding, or omission, of key objects or information, designed to mislead or conceal the truth.

How could Kelly's mom have known what her daughter was up to? Here's how, and what you can do with your daughter to avoid a similar situation:

- Gather more information.

- Trust, but verify by calling the friend she says she's going to be with, or the friend's parent.

- Ask that her friend pick her up at your house.

- Notice if she makes eye contact with you before she exits.

- Be suspicious of sudden sweetness.

- Check her energy level—is it higher than normal or does she appear overly quiet?

- Did she spend more time than usual getting ready?

- Compare and contrast the clothing she would normally wear when the two girls went out before—is there any difference? Or is she carrying a larger purse than usual? It could be that she plans on changing into "date" clothes after she leaves the house.

Developing a healthy relationship with your kids is a key component to get lying under control. If kids feel secure in knowing they can speak openly and honestly and not be shut down or minimized for their feelings or desires, it will go a long way in winning the lying game.

The Least You Need to Know

- Lying is normal for kids to do. This is not typically reason for concern unless it is accompanied by changes in behavior, such as withdrawal, anger, or depression.

- Everyday lies are difficult to detect, and kids may not even see the harm in them.

- High-stakes lies involve risk and reward. Young children are not developmentally capable of making moral decisions. They are motivated by simple needs and desires. They just want to be liked, needed, and included.

- Overreaction encourages deception. Parents should apply consistent consequences but not be hung up on moral judgment.

Chapter 12

Body of Evidence

In This Chapter

- The truth about lies
- Tricks of the trade
- Deception detectives in action

In previous chapters, you learned that there's no single way to tell if a person is lying. Our bodies do give us away, but it takes a whole, well ... body of evidence to do so. In this chapter, you learn what the experts look for when they're trying to determine whether someone is lying.

The ability to detect deception will give you a strategic advantage in negotiations, employee interviews, business relationships, trials, investigations, and everyday life.

These time-tested tips have been used to train law enforcement officers, military intelligence, private investigators, social workers, polygraph examiners, judges, and psychologists.

There are no half-truths or concealment here. We're giving you the real deal as taught by some of the best minds in the business, including Dr. Paul Ekman, the real-life psychologist we've referred to in Part 1, portrayed as Dr. Cal Lightman on the Fox television series *Lie to Me*.

Different Kinds of Lies

Dr. Ekman defines lies as the intention to deliberately mislead, without prior notification of this purpose and without having been explicitly asked to do so by the target. He says there are two primary ways to lie: concealment and falsification. In concealing, the liar withholds information without actually saying anything untrue. In falsifying, the liar withholds true information and presents false information as if it were true.

YA DON'T SAY

Magicians and poker players deceive, but they're not lying, according to Ekman. Liars rely on the presumption of truth. Magic and poker rely on illusion and bluff. If everyone is on notice, the deception is a performance, not a lie. Also, there are no real consequences, i.e., no risk. On the other hand, if a magician were to claim real magical powers, that would be a lie.

That's the view from 30,000 feet, but not all lies are alike. As a deception detective in training, you need to know how different kinds of lies "look" down here at street level. Generally speaking, the bigger the lie, and the more the liar has to lose, the harder it is to avoid detection. There are some interesting exceptions, as you will read, but as a general guideline, this rule holds true. Let's start with an easy one.

High-Stakes Lies

High-stakes lies bear serious exposure consequences—financial, physical, or emotional—from loss of a job or a marriage, all the way up to death row. Think of Bernie Madoff or the late President Richard Nixon.

When a high-stakes liar deviates from the truth, it takes mental energy both to maintain the mechanics of the illusion—keeping their story straight—and to avoid detection. Despite their best efforts, however, the deceptive indicators of a high-stakes liar are so strong that it is almost impossible to conceal them from a trained eye. If our sense of smell was more highly developed, we could probably smell a liar from a mile away.

Day-to-Day Lies

"You look fine." "It's so good to see you!" "Let's do lunch." "I'm well." These are examples of everyday lies, and they are almost impossible to detect because there's nothing to lose or gain in telling the truth.

Self-Deception

Self-deception occurs when the deceiver is unaware they're deceiving themselves, or does not understand the motive for deceiving themselves. This is most often seen in dating relationships, in career ambitions, and on *American Idol*.

> **SAY WHAT?**
>
> A liar has a choice. Presumably, a pathological liar is compelled to lie, and therefore, by my definition, is not a liar.
>
> —Dr. Paul Ekman, psychologist and world leader in the field of facial expressions

Concealment

A lie in sheep's clothing, a concealed truth is deceit by omission. Deceptive concealment occurs when you choose not to reveal something upon direct questioning or fail to proactively disclose information you are contractually obligated to reveal through, say, an employee ethics policy, oath of office, or code of conduct.

For example, if you witness a co-worker stealing company property, and don't follow company policy requiring you to report the theft, that is deceitful concealment. Similarly, if your best friend asks whether her boyfriend has been unfaithful, and you know he has, failing to tell her is deceptive.

Knowing your friend's boyfriend is cheating, and keeping it to yourself until she asks, is not technically a lie, in that you have neither been asked nor are you under any contractual obligation to disclose. However, if you don't tell her, you may want to examine the meaning of your friendship.

Partial Truths

Most liars prefer to conceal, rather than fabricate, because fabrication requires having to remember the false story. If they have to fabricate, more often than not, they'll mix truths with lies to give their deception a more pleasing and believable appearance, like hiding poison in an apple.

> **WORKIN' IT**
>
> If a person makes a false statement without the intention to mislead, then it is not considered a lie; it is simply a mistake. We have all forgotten information or specific details in a situation, therefore, giving a false accounting of events does not constitute a lie. Your demeanor would be consistent with truth-telling.

Tricks of the Trade

Remember from Chapter 1, we covered the steps about reading a person's body language. Now it's time to put those skills to work in detecting deception. Here's a refresher on those steps:

1. Establish rapport: Face-to-face or over the phone, a three- to five-minute warm-up should break the ice.

2. Mirror speech and behavior: Match your words and mannerisms loosely with the person you are observing. Look for signs they are in sync with you.

3. Norming: Observe the person you are studying carefully during these first few minutes of casual conversation. Make note of any nervous quirks or unusual mannerisms to avoid misinterpreting them later during more direct questioning.

4. Find their baseline: These are behaviors you observed during the norming phase, as you were building rapport.

5. Compare and contrast: During questioning, observe and record changes from the baseline.

Remember, you are looking for inconsistencies. There's no one Pinocchio response, no growing liar's nose, but there are lots of ways liars telegraph their deception. When someone is trying to deceive you, you'll notice one or more of the following:

- Facial expressions that don't match words

- Body language that doesn't match voice

- Tone of voice that doesn't match words

- Any variation thereof

In deception detection, we have a term for these verbal and nonverbal anomalies: "hot spots."

SAY WHAT?

He that has eyes to see and ears to hear may convince himself that no mortal can keep a secret. If his lips are silent, he chatters with his fingertips; betrayal oozes out of him at every pore.

—Sigmund Freud

Deceptive Demeanor

Having discovered some valuable items missing from your home, you ask your cleaning person whether she knows anything about it.

Having observed her on several occasions, you notice several changes in her demeanor. Her facial expressions seem anxious and fidgety, but her body movements suggest just the opposite. Normally animated, she typically uses a lot of hand gestures. Today, her hands are still. In fact, her whole body seems overly calm, and her speech patterns are overly solicitous and polite.

You can't say, for certain, that she took the items, but from your observations, it is clear that she is concealing something and that it is leaking out through her body language.

In the workplace, if the boss were to say, "Everything's fine; the company is financially strong," and then take his hand and run it along the inside rim of his shirt collar, you might want to update your résumé.

Running a hand along the collar indicates discomfort and deception.

WORKIN' IT

Body language betrayals generally occur within four seconds of a verbal statement. If it occurs beyond four seconds, the anxiety and the statement are not related.

Here are some other deception clues and what they mean:

- Eye locks are used when trying to convince rather than convey, and/or for intimidation. Other eye clues include excessive blinking (anxiety) and prolonged closure (deceit).

- Body angling away from you suggests a desire to run away or escape an uncomfortable situation.

Angling the body away shows you want to get away from the situation.

- Micro-shoulder shrugs, the body language equivalent of crossed fingers, cancel out words spoken. For example, if a defendant says "I'm innocent," watch for a micro-shoulder shrug on one side of the body or the other, which would suggest just the opposite.

- Anxiety manifests as grooming gestures, adjusting clothing, touching the hair, and rubbing hands or thumbs.

- Inappropriate laughs or smiles are signs of anxiety.

- Hands over the face suggest hiding, or, if a finger is placed over the mouth, a physical reminder to withhold information.

Covering the face suggests withholding information or hiding.

- Barriers are crossing arms or placing an object between yourself and another.

Other clues might include:

- Slumping
- Eye pulling

Eye pulling is a deceptive and boastful gesture.

- Action stance is where the hands are braced on the arms of the chair, and one foot is in front of the other in a running stance that means, "I'm out of here!"

- Rapid posture changes

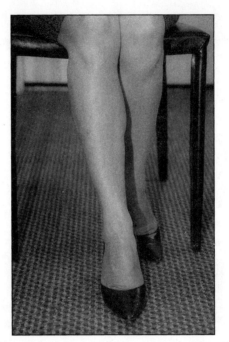

This running stance shows you're ready to get away from the situation.

YA DON'T SAY

When baseball great Alex Rodriguez, the New York Yankees slugger known as A-Rod, was questioned about whether he had used steroids, his answer was, "No," followed by a quick contemptuous expression where one side of his mouth stretched sideways and then released to a relaxed state. When this occurs, the contemptuous mouth gesture cancels out the no and turns it into a yes. Gotcha!

Lack of Illustrators

In Chapters 7 and 8 you learned that illustrators are gestures that add to or fill in the blanks during a conversation. When it comes to spotting lies, a person who generally gestures during conversation, but suddenly stops displaying hand and arm gestures during a specific point in the conversation, might be giving a clue that should be noted and documented to determine the underlying reason.

For example, if your friend Alberto, an Italian from Rome, shares a story about his trip to Kilimanjaro, you would see him gesture with his hands and arms as he describes the adventurous trip. When asked a specific question of where in Kilimanjaro he was, you might notice his hand and arm gestures freeze momentarily. Gotcha!

Duping Delight

There are those who get satisfaction from deceiving others. When they feel they have duped you, and think you fell for it, there is a sense of arousal or delight. This *duping delight* is often accompanied by an inappropriate or awkward smile.

  SAY WHAT?

Duping delight occurs when a deceiver feels exhilaration, joy, pleasure, glee, or satisfaction in deception.

A good example of this would be former Penn State assistant football coach Jerry Sandusky, who smiled his way eerily through a tough interview with television commentator Bob Costas, regarding allegations that Sandusky had molested children. Like crocodile tears, beware of a crocodile smile, smirk, or giggle that seems out of context. That's another gotcha!

Inappropriate smiles are an indicator of duping delight.

Documenting Behavior Clues

Although not always practical, you might consider creating your own abbreviations to document behavior clues, particularly when interviewing job candidates or anytime you have several people you must observe.

The most important thing to remember when doing this is to match up behavior changes with content. For example, when interviewing a new candidate for hire, notice the way they're sitting in the chair, in what direction they're crossing their legs, if they are still or fidgety, and their speech. Look for shifts or changes in behavior.

If the candidate sits with their legs crossed left to right, holding both hands in their lap, and speaking fluidly, this would be their baseline.

During the interview, you notice a gap in their résumé, and politely ask for clarification of employment history between 2010 and 2012. At this time, the prospective employee uncrosses their legs and leans back, crossing their arms. You document the behavior changes on your interviewing pad and next to them write down the dates and content in question.

This will help you pinpoint the hot spots in the résumé. There may a very good reason, such as maternity leave, family illness, or a layoff to explain the gap.

Use the following chart to help you document behaviors. It will help you use abbreviations, rather than writing full words that the employee might pick up on. Feel free to use these abbreviations or create your own.

- Bgr = Breaking gaze to right
- Xarms = Crossing arms
- Xlgs = Crossing legs
- Lcr = Legs crossed right
- Ct = Clearing throat
- Db = Deep breath
- F = Fidgety

- Dete = Direct eye contact
- Er = Early response
- ... = Delayed response
- Gb = Grooming behavior
- Ill = Illustrators
- Lgh = Laugh
- ! = No
- +! = Yes
- Rtg = Repeating the question
- Sn = Scratch neck
- Sic = Shift in chair
- X ... + = Stop and start verbal behavior
- Sd = Strong denial
- Hil = Hands in lap

YA DON'T SAY

Some people can peg a liar 9 times out of 10. These living lie detectors are called "Wizards." Dr. Ekman, and the late Dr. Maureen O'Sullivan, identified less than 50 in 30 years of searching and thousands of people interviewed. Ekman and O'Sullivan began testing for Wizards in the late 1980s. The project was originally dubbed The Diogenes Project, after the Greek philosopher.

The Least You Need to Know

- Lies are falsification or concealment. Deception without the expectation of truth, such as magic or poker, is not a lie. Also, if someone believes their own lies, such as a pathological liar, they are not technically lying, because they believe what they say is the truth.
- The bigger the lie, the easier it is to detect.
- Deception detection is documenting exceptions or measuring deviations from observed normal behavior.
- Establish a baseline for comparing and contrasting behaviors before drawing any conclusions about deception.

Lying Styles

Chapter 13

In This Chapter

- Verbal deception techniques
- Lying by distraction
- Forms of deceptive truths

You've heard the expressions "something's fishy," "something doesn't smell right," or "something doesn't feel right." They all mean the same thing—that someone's story doesn't ring true. It's what we also call a *red herring*.

In this chapter, you learn how to sniff out these lies and distracters like a pro. We examine different ways people dance around the truth, both to hide it and to reveal it—obliquely, when a straight shot might seem harsh, awkward, or unpleasant.

Read My Lips

Warren D. Holmes, a former Miami police detective and authority on interrogation and polygraph examination, lists 12 common ways people try to steer you away from finding out the truth, or throw you off the scent. Although each way has its distinct "smell" and comes into play for a variety of different reasons, they are all forms of distracters or falsifications of a truth.

Argumentum ad Ignorantiam

Argumentum ad ignorantiam is a Latin term meaning "an argument based on an appeal to ignorance." This type of distracter is the old criminal dodge: if you can't prove it, I didn't do it. Remember the phrase from the O. J. Simpson trial: "If the glove doesn't fit, you must acquit." This is a good example of it.

Exaggeration

Tell me if this one sounds familiar: you call in the lowest performer on your sales team to let her know she isn't cutting it, and if she doesn't get back on track, you're going to have to let her go. The words are barely out of your mouth when she fires back: "My numbers are off? The whole economy is off. So why don't you fire the president?"

Instead of taking responsibility for their own performance, the exaggerator will deflect blame by taking the specific—in this case, her performance—and blowing it up or exaggerating it into something beyond their, or your, control.

Argumentum ad Hominem

In Latin, *ad hominem* means "to the man," so *argumentum ad hominem* refers to an argument directed at the person. Have you ever heard a philandering celebrity, exposed by a jilted and/or pregnant lover, deny responsibility by suggesting that the accuser is either a) crazy or b) obsessed? And how many times have we heard political candidates write off an opponent's views as being "socialist," "fascist," or "elitist"?

This common evasive technique allows someone—in this case, the celebrity or politician—to avoid dealing with any substance in the subject matter by attacking the character or credentials of the other party.

Pettifoggery

"Do you bite your thumb at us, sir?"

"I do bite my thumb, sir."

"Do you bite your thumb at us, sir?"

"No, sir, I do not bite my thumb at you, sir; but I bite my thumb, sir."

This classic bit of absurdity from Shakespeare's *Romeo & Juliet* illustrates how a trivial detail can be used to obfuscate the truth—which, in Shakespeare's example, involved the son of a nobleman directing a rude gesture at a member of a rival family, a breach of honor that, no doubt, would have prompted a duel.

This technique, known as *pettifoggery*, is designed to confound the questioner into abandoning a particular line of questioning or blunt the impact of an accusation by burying it in trivial detail. Consider President Clinton's famous "It depends on what your definition of 'is' is" testimony.

SAY WHAT?

Pettifoggery means to quibble over insignificant details. In the later Middle Ages, there was a class of lawyers who earned their livings making a great deal of fuss over minor legal cases. In about 1560, they came to be called pettifoggers. They often had limited concern for scruples or conscience, and the term was deeply contemptuous.

Poisoning the Well

Another favorite of politicians, litigators, and cheating spouses, this dismissive tactic is designed to discredit an accusation without actually denying it. This type of distracter sounds like: "You don't *really* expect them to believe …" And the always popular: "Why would I do something like that? That's just crazy."

YA DON'T SAY

I know a woman who claims she can predict, with 100 percent accuracy, when a man is lying. She says, "Are his lips moving? Then he's lying."

Repeated Assertion

Supercalifragilisticexpiali … *liar!* Mary Poppins was right; if you say something loud enough, and often enough, people start to believe it. Interrogators know this and make a point of not giving a suspect the opportunity to repeat a denial over and over again.

When you hear the same thing over and over again, the liar is often trying to convince everyone else, including themselves, that the lie is in fact the truth.

"You Don't Understand"

Nothing is what it appears to be—at least that's what this type of liar would have you believe. By this reckoning, a con artist becomes a business genius, whose convoluted dealings are just too complex to explain to the likes of you. They'll try to make you believe you'd better sign on now, if you don't want to miss out on the deal of a lifetime. In the case of an adulterer, this tactic is used to become a victim of circumstance. And a bank robber, caught red-handed, might declare, "This isn't what it looks like."

Lying by Referral

Remember what you've already learned about how liars have to work hard to keep their story straight. It gets even harder when that liar has been caught and is questioned. A common tactic to avoid getting tangled in conflicting stories is for the liar to refer you back to a previously told tale, as in, "I already told this to the cops" or "Check your notes." Politicians may cover a lack of specific knowledge, or dodge debate, by saying, "I stand on my record."

The Third-Person Gimmick

Former Senator and one-time presidential candidate Bob Dole liked to speak of himself in the third person. It was a memorable way for him to establish his brand. It was also a little unusual, because most of us have rarely encountered such a thing outside of a queen referring to herself in the plural with the royal "we"—as in, "We are not amused."

In fact, the only other examples that come to mind are Dobby the House Elf from Harry Potter, and maybe an old movie gangster in a stand-off with police, snarling: "You'll never take Tommy Two-Toes alive, see." Liars, narcissists, and used-car dealers will occasionally employ this same self-referential tactic, stepping outside themselves to serve as their own character reference. "Dewey Cheatem wouldn't think of lying to you. Dewey Cheatem's a stand-up guy."

Loophole Lying

A loophole liar isn't sure how much you know. They don't want to get caught in a direct lie, so they'll bracket their lies with those famous words: "to the best of my recollection" or "as I recall." Loophole lying is very common in courtrooms, where a direct lie can lead to a charge of perjury—lying under oath.

The Nonresponsive Liar

A nonresponsive liar borrows time to conjure a lie by stretching out the process. You may hear "Could you say that again" or "What do you mean by that?" Sometimes they'll put the questioner on the defensive by asking things like "Are you calling me a liar?" or "Now why would you say a thing like that?" to throw them off the scent.

Testing the Waters

Anybody old enough to remember Peter Falk as TV detective Lieutenant Columbo knows what deception by testing the waters looks like. In every episode, Columbo would play dumb and keep popping in on the bad guy, asking questions. The bad guy would be fooled into underestimating the detective, and bam! Busted.

On the flipside, a malevolent liar, such as an arsonist, might make regular visits back to the scene of the crime to ask questions, hoping to glean how the investigation is coming along and whether they are a suspect.

 BODY BLOCK

Use caution when you hear someone say, "To tell you the truth," "I swear to God," "To the best of my knowledge," or "I've never told anyone this, but …" Those statements are often followed by a lie.

Deceptive Truths

Your mother probably taught you that if you can't say anything nice, don't say anything at all. If that isn't concealment, I don't know what is. And though not everything concealed is a lie—remember the obligation to disclose—people will often conceal or sugarcoat things to protect your feelings or at least to avoid confrontation. Now we look at some of the ways people say things to let you down easy, and what they really mean.

Al Beback

Anyone who has ever been in sales knows Al Beback, although he's hard to recognize at first. He's that guy who comes in over the lunch hour, or right at closing, and takes up your time asking a bunch of questions. You have all the answers, and you're sure he's going to be reaching for that credit card any minute. That's when he whips off the disguise and declares himself: "I'll be back." And he's gone, along with any hope of ever seeing him again. You curse your luck.

Every salesman knows Al Bebacks never come back. They don't say no thanks or they're not interested, they just take up your time, making you believe they are interested, but then just disappear.

Hints

Couples are notorious for communicating in code—and not bothering to give each other the key. Rather than say what they mean outright, they'll drop what they think are little hints, thinking their meaning, or code, should be crystal clear, when in fact, their partners have no clue.

Okay, sure, a husband could be reasonably expected to know that when his wife says the garbage can is getting full, she means: "Isn't it about time you took out the trash?" But "that darn washing machine keeps eating my socks" does not universally translate to "Honey, I wish you'd do a better job of pairing up my socks when you do the wash."

Innuendo

Innuendos are like jellyfish. They look harmless but can pack a powerful sting. To paraphrase Kanye West: I ain't sayin' she's a gold-digger, but she won't date you if you're broke.

To say someone "has light fingers," for example, is to suggest they'll steal from you like a pickpocket. To suggest that someone may be "a few fries short of a Happy Meal" is to suggest that they might not be right in the head.

Hyperbole

When it comes to deception, hyperbole—a form of exaggeration—is second cousin to innuendo and sister to sarcasm. For example, if someone were to say, "Hey, genius," you can be reasonably certain they're not complimenting you. Hyperbole can also be used as humor, which also distracts you from the truth.

Euphemism

A euphemism is just a wimpy way of saying what you really mean by substituting a nicer word for a hurtful truth. Like when you say someone is "Reubenesque," instead of calling them "fat." If someone says, "Things could be worse," you can be pretty sure they're pretty bad.

The Least You Need to Know

- Misdirection is a form of deception.
- Some liars deflect blame to avoid falsifying the truth.
- Hints and innuendos are deceptive truths.
- Deceptive truths are used to soften harsh reality.

Voice and Vocabulary

14

In This Chapter

- Listening for lies
- LIWC: Linguistic Inquiry and Word Count
- The "I's" have it
- Understanding speech changes

"What's the matter, honey?"

"Nothing."

"It doesn't *sound* like it's nothing."

Does this little exchange sound familiar? You've probably had that exact conversation with someone, which is why you will understand intuitively how much meaning can be conveyed in tone of voice.

We know that the voice can convey emotion, and in this chapter we talk about things experts listen for to determine whether someone is lying. Similarly, a false story, in writing, may look different than the truth. You've no doubt heard the expression: "It's not what you say, it's how you say it." Also in this chapter, you learn that both are important—although maybe not in the ways you might think.

I'm Counting on You

Forget Freud and Rorschach. The hottest thing these days in psychological profiling is Luke—well, LIWC. That's short for Linguistic Inquiry and Word Count, a word-counting and psychological profiling software created by Dr. James W. Pennebaker at the University of Texas, in Austin. Word analysis is like going through an airport checkpoint, where security screeners x-ray you and rummage through the contents of your suitcase. The words you choose, particularly pronouns, and how often you use them offer insight into your personality, social connections, and psychological and physical well-being. Your vocabulary, both written and spoken, offers insight into how you think, how you feel, and who you are.

Pennebaker's exhaustive study of more than half a million letters, poems, books, blogs, conversations, and texts, published in the 1990s, found that people leave word signatures as distinctive as fingerprints. This groundbreaking work has been used recently to study everything from deception to the political temperature of the Arab spring.

WORKIN' IT

Here's a quick English review: Pronouns are words like "I, you, and they." Examples of articles are "a, an, and the." Some prepositions are "to, of, and for." Auxiliary verbs are words like "is, am, and have."

If you'd like to give LIWC a try, Dr. Pennebaker offers some interesting exercises on the website for his book *The Secret Life of Pronouns* (secretlifeofpronouns.com). For now, we will share some of Dr. Pennebaker's findings.

In the next few paragraphs, we offer a cross-section of what Pennebaker calls "function" words—the heart of LIWC analysis—and then we'll test your new knowledge with a real-life example.

The "I" Word

It's the most common word in the English language. (Let's face it, we're all full of ourselves.) And so it follows that I-words track where people pay attention. Dr. Pennebaker says people who are self-focused, insecure, or self-effacing, tend to use first-person singular pronouns (I, me, my) at high rates.

Confident, task-focused folks let the I-words drop—of course, so do liars, which is where things get interesting:

- Women tend to use I-words more than men.

- Poor people tend to use more I-words than the rich.

- Depressed people use more I-words than happy people.

- The young use more I-words than the elderly.

All of that tends to have a fairly negative connotation, but research has also shown that people who use more personal pronouns also tend to be telling the truth. Context, of course, is key.

Other Revealing Words

I-words are also known as "self-referential" words. Here are other function words and what they reveal about someone:

Social words: They, she, us, we, talk, and friends; these words tend to be used more often by people who are more social and enjoy close relationships.

Positive emotion words: Love, happy, great, or good; these are the words of people who see the world in a positive light.

Negative emotion words: Hate, disgust, kill, afraid, and sad; these words are the vocabulary of the neurotic and people who tend to see life through tainted lenses.

Big words: People who use lots of words longer than six letters tend to be more educated but also may be more detached and emotionally distant.

LIWC and Lying

Any fiction writer will tell you that making things up isn't as easy as you might think. Making up a story about something you haven't actually experienced and passing it off as true, or at least believable, is a skill few possess. Most liars give themselves away—either through words that don't match their expressions or through the words themselves.

Dr. Pennebaker turned his linguistic inquiry and word-counting skills on himself, analyzing recommendation letters he'd written for students. An interesting pattern developed. Letters for the students he held in highest regard tended to have fewer positive emotion words and more concrete facts. Conversely, letters for weaker students tended to focus more on the reader, "I'm sure you will find …" and less on the student.

He also tended to write more about the better students, because he had more to work with. Similarly, Pennebaker writes that liars will generally write and say less, because they have fewer "real" details to reveal. He notes that real stories used more personal pronouns and fewer emotion words. Also, real stories have more words that describe time, space, and movement, and use fewer verbs and cognitive (thinking) words.

When it comes to deception, beware of people who use "would, should, could, and ought"; these discrepancy verbs imply imagined rather than actual experience. Interestingly, these are the very words fiction writers are taught to eliminate from their vocabulary, to give their work a more realistic tone.

YA DON'T SAY

Polygraph test results are not admissible in court. The reason? These so-called "lie detectors" have been proven to be wrong more than 40 percent of the time.

The following graph demonstrates words associated with honesty and deception.

Words Associated with Honesty and Deception

	Deception	Mixed	Honesty

Self-reference
  I-words

Cognitive complexity
  Word/sentence.
  Word count
  Big words
  Insight words
  Conjunctions
  Exclusives

Detailed information
  Relativity
  Time
  Space
  Motion
  Numbers
  Quantifiers
  Prepositions
  Negations
  Causal words
  Articles

Social and emotional references
  Social words
  You
  She, he, they
  We
  It, any, those
  Positive emotions
  Negative emotions

Verbs
  Total verbs
  Auxiliary verbs
  Discrepancies

Note that words with bars on the left side of the table are reliably associated with deception. The further to the left, the less trustworthy. Those on the right side are markers of honesty. Those words with bars close to the center line are not reliably associated with either truth or deception.

Words associated with honesty and deception.
(Courtesy of Dr. James W. Pennebaker, author, *The Secret Life of Pronouns: What Our Words Say About Us*; and founder of LIWC)

How You Say It

Because liars spend time and energy making up a story, they will often lose track of what their voice is giving away. It is almost impossible to control voice, words, body language, and facial expressions all at once, so clues will leak out in the places they're unable to control. It's like patting your head while rubbing your belly and hopping on one foot, all at the same time.

Here are some "leaks" to look for, and what they reveal:

- Rapid speech: verbal adrenaline response, anxiety, fight or flight
- Increased voice volume: stress
- Higher pitch: fear, anxiety
- Pauses between the words: distraction, preoccupation, concentration
- Hesitation at the beginning of the speaker's turn: calculation, reflection, weighing options
- Uh, um, ah: stalling for time
- Repeating words: another stalling tactic
- Unfinished words: preoccupation, uncertainty
- Broken speech: scrambling for words

Vocal *errors* occur when the deceiver isn't prepared to answer questions. They stammer around until their brain kicks in to conjure up a response.

Speech errors can also occur when someone is well-rehearsed. They may practice their lines ahead of time, but when it comes to crunchtime, they freeze up, which causes speech errors and hesitations in the flow of the conversation.

You may be thinking, "That has happened to me before, and I wasn't lying; I was just nervous speaking in front of others." That's correct; someone can be truthful and have the same symptoms as lying. You have to rely on context clues to rule out normal nervousness versus getting your story straight. That's why establishing a baseline is so important.

SAY WHAT?

Error is a phenomenon where a person who appears deceptive can be completely truthful, but due to one's fear of being disbelieved, will have the same responses as a deceptive person.

Inflection

Speech inflection is the pitch plus loudness of voice. When someone's voice becomes louder and the pitch goes up, it suggests the presence of underlying fear or anger. The question you, as a deception detective, have to ask yourself is: why?

For example, if your spouse returns home late without prior warning, you might ask, "Honey, where have you been?" If his voice becomes louder than normal and the pitch goes up, there is an underlying cause. First, rule out problems at work or other issues, before jumping to conclusions. If he says everything's okay at work, then it's reasonable to suspect there's something going on that he doesn't want you to know about.

Pace

Pace is the speed with which thoughts are communicated through speech. A liar, put on the spot, will experience an adrenaline rush—the old "fight or flight" instinct. This often manifests as accelerated speech. The old saying, "Beware of fast-talkers," isn't far from the truth.

Lowered Voice

A liar's voice may also become softer when disguising a lie, as if they're telling a secret. Have you ever found yourself suddenly lowering your voice when talking with a friend, even though there's no one around to hear? Subconsciously, you hit the mute button because you knew that the information you were about to share was either partially untrue or something you shouldn't be sharing.

Mumbling

Some liars may intentionally mumble specific facts, or cover their mouths when talking, to keep you from hearing specific details. It's the verbal equivalent of the small print in contracts.

Buying Time

A classic stalling tactic is that of buying time to conjure up a response to cover a lie. A savvy liar will be able to come up with a quicker answer than an unskilled liar. Nevertheless, there will always be a delay in the response, some longer than others, based on the liar's intellectual capacity. If someone can't seem to pull off a big fat lie, they'll pair a little truth with a lie.

Monotone

The flat-line, monotone voice may indicate a skillful liar concealing emotions. A skillful liar thinks that if they appear to be in control and avoids showing any emotion, their lies will appear more believable. Clearly, if someone always speaks in a monotone, then that would be considered their norm and should not be counted as deception. If monotone is not their normal mode of communication, something is probably up.

Laughing

Deception is no laughing matter, but laughter can be a sign of deception. Unlike spontaneous laughter, which is a natural body response, fake laughter is manipulative. Spontaneous laughter is accompanied by a heartfelt smile, as discussed in Chapter 4, where the corners of the mouth turn up and the cheeks rise, causing crow's feet to appear around the eyes. A fake laugh may be accompanied by a forced smile, where the mouth turns up and stretches horizontally, avoiding crow's feet. It's almost as if smiling is painful.

Just because a laugh is spontaneous doesn't always mean it's a good thing. Laughter before or after a statement can be an indicator of deception or nervousness.

When you hear giggles during a conversation, but there's nothing to laugh about, you have to question what they are saying that would make them feel uncomfortable enough to cover it with a laugh.

> **WORKIN' IT**
>
> Clues that may indicate deception: smiling and voice pitch change; no smile, with increased voice pitch; no change in pitch, but a forced smile is detected; or no pitch or smile.

The Least You Need to Know

- The pronouns someone uses and the frequency they use them can reveal the truth.
- Thare are voice changes in tone and tempo when someone is lying.
- Liars work hard to lie and pay less attention to their speech patterns and voice, which actually can reveal they are lying.
- Awkward smiling and laughing can be signs of deception.

Strictly Business

What if you could learn to how have the confidence, and the body language skills, to convince any employer that you're perfect for the job? We'll show you how, along with how to read the signals to tell when an interview is going well, or not well, and how make instant changes to get it back on track.

This part also explores how to use your position onstage and spatial anchoring to make persuasive presentations. And speaking of persuasion, you'll learn negotiation signals that will instantly convey the emotions behind common gestures, as well as how to resolve conflicts soon after they arise.

Because the most important business of all is the business of personal relationships, this book ends with discussions of how to tell if someone is attracted to you, and how to convey your own feelings and desires through body language.

Body Language for Job Interviews

In This Chapter

- How your body language can get you the job
- What the do's and don'ts are in an interview
- How to read the signals of the interviewer

Landing a great job not only takes having a great résumé of experience, it takes having a great interview. A great interview happens with body language that communicates "I'm the one for the job." Your level of confidence, professionalism, self-esteem, and many other characteristics are signaled to a potential employer before you ever answer that first interview question.

This chapter explains how to prepare for and execute a successful interview. You also learn to read the signals of how you're doing.

How to Dazzle a Potential Employer

You've learned the power of a great first impression, and in a job interview, the first impression you make can be the difference between what gets you hired and what sends you packing. If you want to impress an employer, it takes the right look, walk, posture, and gestures—and résumé and experience, of course—to nail the interview.

Let's explore how to put all the techniques you've learned about body language into play to get you the job you really want. We'll walk through an interview step by step.

Do Your Homework

In preparation for your interview, learn as much as you can about the company you're interviewing with. Search their website; read customer reviews; and research competing companies and the industry. This preparation will ultimately give you confidence that will show in your body language, and you will be prepared for any questions that may arise.

The Waiting Area

While you're waiting in the lobby, avoid making or receiving phone calls, and don't search your email messages and texts on your phone. Opt for reading the company's brochures and reading materials instead. It shows you are interested in being there and not preoccupied with something else. Plus, the gatekeeper at the front desk will inevitably notice what you're doing, so make even those first minutes in the building count.

Travel Light

When you walk into a potential employer's office, only carry the bare essentials, such as your résumé and personal planner; leave the rest in your car. Bulky handbags, backpacks, or large leather briefcases send the wrong message and can signal blockage between you and the interviewer. Keep it simple and organized to streamline your image. Also, avoid carrying a cup of coffee or soft drink into the interview—it's another distracter.

Left: Travel with the bare minimum for your interview.
Right: Carrying a bunch of papers as well as a bulky bag can make you appear
disorganized to the interviewer.

Dress Accordingly

These grooming tips will help you communicate a professional and well-maintained demeanor:

- Avoid heavy perfumes and colognes; opt for a very mild body lotion or after-shower spray.

- Avoid long shoulder-strap purses, and if you must carry a handbag, opt for a small- to medium-sized handheld one.

- Men should polish their shoes and wear a matching belt.

- Ladies should pull up or back long hair; it's more professional, and it will help you avoid the urge to touch your hair or face during the interview.

- Men should shave the fur around their neck collar and ears. No one likes to see a Chia Pet growing back there.

- Ladies should avoid figure-hugging clothes, skirts shorter than 2 inches above the knee, and displays of cleavage. Keep it professional.

- Ladies should wear light makeup and natural-colored lipstick.

- Both men and women should get a manicure with a natural finish and color for a clean, well-maintained look.

- If possible, whiten your teeth.

Meet and Greet

When you first meet the person who you'll be interviewing with, remember the confident handshake rule, and follow it. Give the prospective employer a genuine smile and maintain appropriate eye contact.

Entering the Interview

When you enter the employer's office, close the door behind you but never turn back toward the door, breaking face with the employer. This breaks the connection you've made with the interviewer before you even sit down.

If you've ever had a massage, you've noticed that when the masseuse moves from one side of the customer to the other, they always place one hand on the customer's back and move to the other side without breaking contact. It's the same idea.

The proper way to enter your future employer's office is to walk a step or two into the room while holding onto the doorknob, shift hands, and close the door with the other hand while maintaining eye contact.

If the interviewer enters first, just make sure you are facing the employer. The point is to try not to break eye contact or turn your back on the interviewer.

Left: Don't turn your back to the interviewer when shutting the door.
Right: Keep your connection to the interviewer while shutting the door.

Men, when you're seated, place your feet shoulder-width apart and firmly plant them on the floor; avoid crossing your legs.

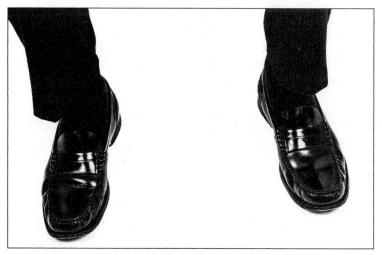

Men should keep their feet planted on the floor.

Women, lean your legs to one side or cross your legs like a lady; avoid crossing your legs at the ankles.

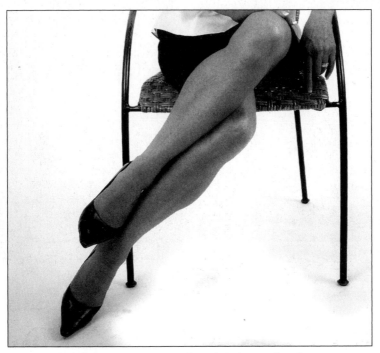

Women should cross or lean their legs to the side.

Hand Placement

Always place your hands in plain view of the employer. Hands in your lap are acceptable only if the employer can see them. Often, when your hands are placed on your lap, they are hidden from view due to the employer's desk height. Always keep your hands out in front, or on the table, if you're meeting in a conference room.

Left: Don't keep your hands under the table.
Right: Do place your hands in sight of the employer.

Level Eyes

Adjust your stance when seated to meet your employer as close to eye level as possible. When you do this, you'll be taken more seriously.

This is true for men as well. If you're taller than your interviewer, adjust your seat lower to avoid overpowering the boss, especially if she's female.

Situate yourself at eye level with the interviewer.

Sitting at higher level than the employer can be seen as overpowering.

Saving Face

Keep a neutral, natural expression on your face, and follow your employer's lead. If they tell a joke, laugh a little, but not too much. Over-gesturing with facial expressions usually sends mixed messages, so keep your face in check.

A neutral expression such as this helps the interviewer take you seriously.

Try to avoid being overexpressive.

Frame It

When speaking, keep your hands and arms within your frame. This means you should keep your hands and arms between your shoulders and hips when gesturing. If you go outside the frame, you'll appear less credible.

Keeping your gestures within frame shows honesty.

Nod Your Head

On specific points of interest, nodding your head sends the signal to the employer that you get it and are agreeable. But avoid the constant head-bobble; it makes you appear insecure and overly agreeable.

Use Color

Find out what the company's colors are from their logos and print materials. Men can accessorize their suit with a tie that has the company's colors in it; and women can wear a pin or scarf with the company's colors. This sends a subliminal message that you're part of the team.

Signs Your Interview Is Headed South

It's important to notice when an interview isn't going well and to make adjustments to salvage it. Here are some tips on how to get things back on track.

Leaning Back

When the employer leans back, it can either signal, "I've made up my mind," or that they have checked out. Be sure to watch for other clues to determine the difference.

Leaning back could mean the interviewer has either made a decision or is bored—pay attention to the clues!

Checking the Time

When an interviewer checks their watch, it sends the signal, "I'm bored, and this interview is over. Next!" Likewise, you shouldn't check your watch during an interview either; it sends a signal that you have somewhere else you'd rather be.

Checking the time signals disinterest.

A Critical Eye

When one eyebrow—or both—rises, an interviewer is signaling that they're not really sold on you and you're under examination.

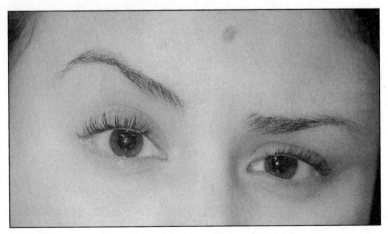

This look signals you are being examined.

Body Angles

When the interviewer's shoulders, legs, or feet face toward the door, they're signaling that they're ready to move on. Also, you shouldn't position your body toward the door because it communicates you're ready to go instead of interested in staying however long it takes.

The Blank Stare

An interviewer is not convinced that you're the right candidate if you observe a blank stare in their eyes. Even if they're just zoning out after a carb-loaded lunch, try to bring them back to the table by changing the topic and re-engaging their interest.

You're Out

When an interview ends abruptly, and the interviewer shakes your hand and avoids eye contact, you're probably out of the running. Notice what happened just before this interaction, and avoid it at future interviews.

You're probably not in the running for the job if the interviewer won't make eye contact when saying good-bye.

Signs the Interview Is Going Well

On the other hand, there is interviewing body language that is very positive, signaling interest and next steps:

Leaning in: When the interviewer leans forward and is actively listening to what you are saying, this can be a sign things are going well and the interviewer is interested in what you have to say. When the lean-in happens, make what you're saying really count.

Happy feet: Both the interviewer's feet are tapping, also known as "happy feet"—this is a good sign!

Tour guide: The interviewer goes into "tour guide" mode and introduces you to the staff.

All smiles: They smile and appear upbeat.

Pleasantly surprised: The employer raises both eyebrows, followed by a smile—they're pleasantly surprised.

Deal: The interviewer shakes your hand, makes eye contact, and seals the deal with a shoulder pat—you're in!

This positive body language from the interviewer would signal that the interview went well.

The Least You Need to Know

- How you groom and dress yourself speaks volumes in a job interview.
- Maintain the connection with your interviewer through eye contact and body position.
- Never check your watch during an interview, and if the interviewer does it, it may not be a good sign for you.
- Good signs during an interview include leaning in, introducing you to others, and a handshake with a shoulder pat.

Body Language of Leaders

Chapter 16

In This Chapter

- Why to use the art of "Suggestology"
- How to give a winning, persuasive presentation
- How to evoke the response you want with hand gestures
- Why to let spatial anchoring work for you

In Part 3, you learned how to examine other people's words and read their voices. Now we use similar techniques to learn how expert leaders can get you to run down the aisle, open your wallet, give up your Saturday, or buy their latest product. In this chapter, you learn how leaders not only use their voices and words to persuade, but also how they use gestures and physical space to lead, motivate, and inspire you. This chapter takes you from being a mediocre leader to an exceptional one with only a few steps and simple techniques.

Suggestology

How do charismatic leaders persuade us to change our views, volunteer our time, open our wallets, and even make us believe that what they want us to do is what we wanted to do in the first place? You've seen it happen to others. You've even been a victim of it yourself, and you've wondered how in the world they do it, time and again. How the heck can we learn to be that convincing?

Passion plus power is an explosive combination, when used properly. Let's coin a phrase to describe this powerful persuasion: "Suggestology." Motivational speakers, television evangelists, and political candidates are pros at it. And you can become an expert Suggestologist, too. Whether your next presentation is to a packed auditorium or to a couple of people over coffee, we show you how to hit it out of the park.

Making a Persuasive Presentation

When you have the opportunity to deliver a presentation, it's your chance to shine. It's your opportunity to go from being average to exceptional, even memorable. The following seven steps will show you how to use your body language and delivery in ways that will engage your audience and get them fired up and on board with what you have to say. We'll use a scenario to demonstrate this seven-step technique.

But first, let's discuss a key component called spatial anchoring and understand how it works in persuasive presentations.

Spatial anchoring is when a speaker chooses one side of the speaking platform on which to deliver the bad news about their business or subject, with excruciating pain. On the opposite side, the speaker delivers all of the good news, and the fact that there's a solution to the problem. The center stage is where the speaker delivers the plan and action steps, and the close. The speaker is anchoring their message by utilizing space, and their voice and words become powerful triggers to move the audience's emotions.

BODY BLOCK

Do not send mixed messages by switching "good" and "bad" sides of your presentation midstream, or you'll lose the effect on your audience.

Now, let's assume you've been selected by your boss to give a presentation to the company's 500 employees to kick-start next year's sales efforts. He explains that it's your job to rally the team; explain the company's goals, objectives, and expectations; get their buy-in; and send them off, fired up and running to sell, sell, sell.

Step 1: Welcome

Begin by welcoming your audience to the sales conference in an upbeat and confident manner. "Welcome everyone to Widget World's Annual Sales Meeting. We are glad you all are here, as this promises to be an exciting start to an exciting year of record-breaking sales." You are making your first, all-important impression here, so make your first words and how you deliver them count.

Step 2: Introductions

Next, tell your audience who you are and why you are there. Again, confidence is key. "I'm John White, Vice President of Sales, and I'm here today to show you exactly how each and every one of you is not only going to meet, but beat your sales goals this year."

Step 3: Participation Prompts

Now, ask your audience two questions to get them engaged. When you ask your questions, raise your hand to "suggest" or "prompt" the audience to follow you by raising their hands to respond to the questions:

1. "How many of you would like to make enough money this year to take your family on a dream vacation?"

   (They all raise their hands.)

   "Great!"

2. "How many of you would like to receive a nice, fat bonus this year for all your hard work and dedication?"

   Again raise your hand while asking the question. This shows you'd like a bonus, too. You're one of them now.

   They'll all raise their hands again.

   "Fantastic! Thank you." Always show your audience that you appreciate them.

Step 4: Spatial Anchoring—The Bad News

Now, before you jump into telling the employees what they need to do to earn their great bonuses and dream vacations, you have to let them experience discomfort first. So here's where spatial anchoring comes into play in your presentation. You must share how the weakened economy has affected the company's profit margin and its viability to survive. When you do this, you use one side of the stage and its space to evoke a feeling of pain.

WORKIN' IT

Before you give an audience the solution to a problem, they first need to experience the pain of not having the solution.

Walk to the left side of the stage. Stop and anchor your feet in one place, then deliver the bad news:

"Ladies and gentleman, it's been a tough couple of years. We've had to close 8 of our 10 offices. I don't have to remind you of the impact this has had on you and your families. I know some of you have had a tough time paying for your kids' college educations, you haven't been taking those memorable family vacations, and some of you have dropped your health insurance just to stay afloat. It's been hard for all of us."

Step 5: Spatial Anchoring—The Good News

Next, you walk to the right side of the stage and stop; anchor your stance, pause for a second or two, and then begin speaking.

"But we have survived! We are still here; stronger than ever, with new hope and expectations for a very profitable year. (Speed up the tempo of your voice.) Your dedication, your perseverance, and your commitment are why we are standing strong! We have exciting plans to share with you today that will allow you to get your kids back in college, allow your family to take that vacation you've been putting off, and start you rebuilding your nest-egg for the future."

> **YA DON'T SAY**
>
> Have you noticed Jay Leno take his stance on center stage, in the exact spot each time, and puts one hand in his pocket? This is a trigger for the audience to laugh. And they do.

Step 6: Center Stage

Center stage is where you'll deliver the plan for the year. To get your audience's participation, use the "cooperation" hand gesture you learned by placing both hands as if gripping an imaginary basketball. This anchors cooperation from the audience.

As you deliver the details of the sales plan, these body language tools will help:

- Use hand gestures to communicate timelines and to accentuate points. For example: "We were here two years ago, and now we're here." (Use space to separate the timelines.)

Help others pick up on timelines and important points with hand gestures.

- Make three to five points of expectations using your fingers. Begin by pointing your forefinger at eye level at the first one, adding your middle finger at the second, and then adding your ring finger at the third. Also, always use odd numbers as a total.

Use your forefinger for the first expectation.

Add your middle finger for the second expectation.

Add your ring finger for the third expectation.

- Drive your message home with a closed fist, thumb on top, on specific points.

- Move your audience's emotions by telling a personal story. Use a momentary hand-over-the-heart gesture, tilt your head down slightly, and speak in a softer voice. Take longer pauses, and draw out specific words.

- Use the A-okay gesture with both hands as a symbol of reassurance during touchy points.

- Motivate your audience by using large, rolling, rapid hand and arm gestures to create action and urgency. Increase the power and influence in your tone by increasing the loudness and pace of your voice.

- Use a "bridging the gap" gesture, made by holding your fingers together, thumbs up, facing hand-to-hand with a V-shaped space in between. This is often seen in political speeches, as an attempt to bring opposing parties together. This gesture is also interpreted as a gate-keeping gesture.

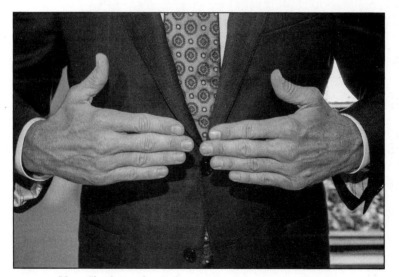

Use a "bridging the gap" gesture to encourage togetherness.

- Inspire by holding both hands up and out, in an open prayer gesture.

Holding hands in an open prayer gesture is a sign of inspiration to others.

Step 7: The Close

In the closing of your presentation, you want to revisit each area of the stage to bring your message full circle. So after the body of your presentation is delivered from center stage, move back to the left side of the stage and anchor the problems you've discussed; review how bad it was; and recall the pain. Then move back to the right side of the stage and review the good news that there can be, and will be, a marvelous future for everyone, with the audience's cooperation and support. Move back to center stage where you anchor the plan to get there.

Remember, this is your big finish. Be clear. Be passionate. Crystalize everything you've said. Tie up everything with a big bow. Finish with a strong quote, your tag line—something that will replay in their minds after they leave.

Then wait. Let your words sink in. And wait for the audience to respond.

WORKIN' IT

The seven-step technique can be used while seated by using right- and left-hand gesturing to anchor your messages. For those who do business negotiations over the phone, use your voice inflection, tone, and pace to separate the good news from the bad.

The Least You Need to Know

- A good speaker utilizes various techniques to inspire, energize, and convince an audience.
- You can make visual suggestions to your audience by making the gesture you want them to emulate.
- Withhold the solution to problems until you've first given your audience time to feel the pain of the problems.
- Spatial anchoring ties audience response to a certain place on the stage.

Negotiation Signals

In This Chapter

- How conflicting body language betrays internal conflict
- How to recognize signals during negotiations
- How to resolve conflict
- How to get cooperation

After you've started your own business or landed your dream job, negotiation skills will be vitally important to your success. Your growing ability to read body language will serve you well, because it is an intricate part of any negotiation.

Many of the body language signals in negotiations mirror the signals you'd look for in any interaction. We've touched on many of these "tells," in different contexts, in previous chapters. In this chapter, we explain how to tell when negotiations are headed south, and how to turn them around.

The Trump Card

Donald Trump is a master of negotiation, and he has a technique all his own. Did you think "The Donald" was seriously considering running for president in 2011? Trump's body language sent mixed messages, so let's take a closer look.

When asked if he was going to run for president, Donald Trump replied, "I think I may run for president." At that precise moment, he affirmed with a small head nod ("yes") followed by licking his lips and swallowing, indicating that this was a big decision, but yes, he was considering it.

Here's a clue that contradicts his words. During one interview, Trump leaned forward with his hands between his knees, resting his forearms on his mid-thigh, with his hands in a low steeple position, fingers pointing to the ground. At the exact moment when Trump was asked if he planned to run, he tapped his thumbs together, synchronized with the beat of his words, meaning he was contemplating running.

So what does this all mean?

The low steeple, the swallowing, the licking of the lips, and the tapping of the thumbs on beat were indicators that he was conflicted; it was a huge undertaking, yet he was contemplating running. The low steeple contradicted any confidence in his ability to win the presidency. Later, in fact, he decided not to run.

These gestures indicate low expectations.

Like Trump's downward-pointing fingers signaling an unconscious expectation of defeat, here are other "tells" of body language in a business setting.

Tap Dancing

You're at the negotiation table, looking across at your opponent's expressionless face. Their hands are crossed, motionless, on the table-top. They appear confident at first glance, but you notice their shoulders and the back of the chair are slightly vibrating. Their stone-faced expression and calm exterior are betrayed by the tap dance of their feet under the table. They're concealing anxiety, and tap-dancing feet can also signal the following:

- Anticipation
- Boredom
- Nervousness

Rocking

When you feel like you've got a big fish on the hook or a good deal in the making, you may find yourself rocking back and forth on both feet like a see-saw. Watch for this in who you're negotiating with as well; it can indicate they think they have you where they want you.

Rubbing Hands Together

When you rub your hands together in a negotiation, it means, "This is going to be good!" This actions signals anticipation that is positive.

Grooming Gestures

When you touch your hair, adjust your clothes, pull on your shirt cuffs, or rub your arms or legs, these are actually self-soothing ges-tures. This is anxiety leaking out.

Karate Chop

Vertical slashing with the hand—almost as if it were a meat cleaver—is a gesture to be taken seriously; it's the silent equivalent of "It's my way or the highway." This is frequently used for emphasis. It's the gesture Donald Trump uses in his television show, *The Apprentice*, when he says: "You're fired!"

You're fired!

Finger Pointing

When someone points a finger at you, at someone else, or in a particular direction, they may be bullying or playing the blame game.

Finger pointing is a bullying gesture.

Face Scratching

When someone reaches with one hand across their face to scratch the other side with the thumb or fingers, this can be a signal of deception. This deal may not be on the up-and-up.

This gesture can indicate a dirty deal.

Pupil Dilation

When a deal looks or feels good to someone, their pupils will dilate. When a deal smells bad, you may notice their pupils constrict.

Ring Around the Collar

Running your finger around the inside of your collar shows discomfort. In other words, it's getting hot in here!

The heat is on!

Flared Nostrils

Flared nostrils are a body language indication of either anger or arousal. Depending on the person, this could mean things are going well or going south.

Flared nostrils can be a sign of anger.

Wedding Ring Twist

When someone twists their wedding ring around and around their finger, it's a signal about their spouse. They're worried about what their spouse's response will be to what's being discussed.

Twisting your wedding ring around your finger signals spousal conflict.

Squirming

Shifting, squirming, or changing body position can indicate a variety of internal conflict concerns including irritation, frustration, fear, or even deception.

Internal conflict is apparent when you squirm or are unable to get comfortable.

Leaning Away

Resistance is expressed in body language by leaning back or away, with folded arms. Pulling on an ear or the nose also expresses resistance.

Reserving Judgment

When you place a hand over your mouth with a clasped palm around your chin, you may be reserving judgment, or it may indicate deception.

This gesture either shows you are reserving judgment or being deceptive.

Critical Thinking

A person with their hand resting on their cheek, with their forefinger up, is thinking critically.

The hand resting on the cheek in this manner indicates a critical thinker.

Chin Stroking

Stroking of the chin means a person is evaluating something and thinking about it.

You appear to be evaluating someone or something when you stroke your chin.

Steeple

When someone makes a steeple shape with their fingers, they are usually making or about to make a factual, expert, or profound statement.

Steepling of the fingers is the sign of an expert.

Closed Hand Gestures

Making gestures with a closed hand means you may be feeling insecure or could be hiding something.

You may also be timid or feeling uneasy if you use this gesture.

What Am I Thinking?

Let's test what we've learned so far in this chapter.

Look at the following photo and determine what each team member
is thinking. Begin by determining who you think the CEO of the
company is. Keep in mind there are those in the photo who fit more
than one emotion.

Take a quick glance overall, and then study each person to see what
clues you can pick up. Take into consideration the expressions on
their faces, their body language—the angles of their shoulders,
hands, and arms. Match the following emotions to the people in the
photo (note: there may be more than one answer for each person):

- Engaged
- Suspicious
- Guarded
- Anxious

- Angry
- Skeptical
- Disengaged

What are they thinking?

Check your answers in Appendix B.

Gaining Cooperation

One place you don't want to experience resistance is at work. Here's how can you gain cooperation using a few body language concepts.

Seating Arrangements

Something as simple as the seating arrangement at the conference table can influence the level of cooperation your team experiences. When you want cooperation from your team members, the best place to sit at the conference table is midway down the table on either side. Avoid the head and foot of the table; these positions indicate taking charge. When the leader seeks cooperation, they become part of the team.

Conflict Resolution

Let's assume you're sitting at the conference table negotiating with clients, and a conflict develops between your best sales guy and your client's attorney. Gauging the temperature in the room at this point is crucial, so stay alert.

You feel the chill in the air as your client disengages. You read their blank stare. Are they uninterested or frustrated? And how do you re-engage their interest?

The first error most negotiators make is to talk too much. You learn more when others are talking. So button it up and encourage your client to talk. Here's how:

- Lean forward; tilt your head slightly and make genuine eye contact; nod your head on a major point to assure the client you got the message.

- Change the topic. You can't change your client's state of mind by repeating the same points on the same topic. Look for common ground.

- Encourage your client to adjust their stance by sharing a story, showing them photos, or giving a testimonial.

- If the client appears fidgety, take a break and walk together to the coffee machine. Walking and talking can release tension. If you can, take a walk outside. A change of scenery can sometimes adjust an attitude for the better.

WORKIN' IT

A quick remedy to gain a client's cooperation is to keep them talking; the more information you gather, the easier it is to pinpoint the client's concerns and needs. Instead of asking specific questions, get them to answer their own by using minimal encouragers, including using words such as and, then, so, what, really, and hmmm; hitchhiking off the words they use; or repeating the tail end of their sentences.

Using Minimal Encouragers

Here's a scenario demonstrating how minimal encouragers can help work through someone's conflict in a negotiation:

Salesperson: Aren't these kitchen appliances beautiful?

Customer: They're perfect. But money's tight right now.

Salesperson: Right now?

Customer: Yes, I have my daughter's college tuition coming due.

Salesperson: Really?

Customer: Yes, so right now new appliances are out of our budget.

Salesperson: But …

Customer: We would love to buy new appliances, but not right now.

Salesperson: Not right now?

Customer: Yes, maybe in the fall.

Salesperson: In the fall?

Customer: In the fall, we will be in a better place financially to make a purchase.

Salesperson: And …

Customer: We'll be ready to buy then.

Salesperson: Great! You know, we can set up a payment plan for 12 months, interest-free, and your first payment won't begin until fall. This way, you won't have to wait for your new kitchen; you can take all your new appliances home today.

Customer: That's fantastic; let's do it!

Putting It All Together

Following are three photos of one-on-one business encounters. With the techniques you have learned throughout this book, identify the clues suggested by the client's body language and select a strategy to answer the client's questions and close the deal.

Negotiation 1.

Negotiation 2.

Negotiation 3.

- Do you need to go back and build rapport?
- Address the clients' concerns that you see written on their faces.
- Identify your customer's communication and learning styles.
- Is your client withholding information? Can you use minimal encouragers to get them to open up?
- Are they telling you the truth?
- Listen to their voice tone and pace and the words they select.
- Are they giving you excuses?

In this book, you learned how to read facial expressions; identify the meanings of gestures, and interpret body language, voice, and words. Now that you have the foundation, use the skills to identify the spoken and unspoken clues your customers, colleagues, opponents, and friends are giving you, to interpret what they are really saying.

If you see frustration in one face, it means you'll need to clarify information. If you see sadness or pain, then it's a clue there is some emotional issue that needs to be addressed before you can move forward. If a client appears disengaged or vacant, that is a clue that you need to change your strategy to reel them back in. If they're leaning away, back, or toward the exit door, you've lost them; so you'll need to use your rapport-building and communications skills to realign them. The answers and solutions are literally right before your eyes.

The Least You Need to Know

- Pay attention to inconsistencies between spoken words and contradictory body language.
- Negotiations can be enhanced by careful attention to body language clues.
- Conflict resolution is often a matter of reading body language and changing tactics quickly and accordingly.
- Minimal encouragers can help a client answer and overcome their own objections.

The Language of Attraction

Chapter 18

In This Chapter

- The signals of attraction
- Eye gazing techniques
- Do's and don'ts of flirtation and dating

In the blink of an eye, you can meet your dream partner. And when that happens, you'll want your body language to be communicating the way you want it to, because it's going to be doing most of the talking anyway.

You learned in prior chapters that the key to any successful personal or professional encounter is eye contact. But did you know that connecting with your eyes is on the top 10 list of ways to make someone fall in love with you? In this chapter, you learn how to connect with someone using eye gazing techniques, and recognize flirtation signals and use them. We also explain some dating do's and don'ts to help you successfully send and read the signals.

Open Your Eyes

Has this ever happened to you? The hottest person you've ever seen is walking right toward you. Your heart begins to race, the excitement builds, and then, Oh no! They walk right on by, never glancing your way or acknowledging that you exist.

"How did that just happen?" you ask yourself. Maybe you feel like you're wearing garlic around your neck, warding off everyone in your path. Perhaps you begin to second-guess yourself. You may wonder, "Am I losing my edge? And if so, how do I get it back?"

Perhaps you should look in the mirror and do a self-evaluation. Are you slouched over, disheveled, looking down or away? If so, then you shouldn't be surprised that your dream date walked right by. Your body language didn't exactly say you are someone they should take interest in.

Even with online dating all the rage, at some point you will have to meet a potential mate face to face. When that happens, don't let the opportunity to connect with someone great get away by not being prepared with the body language of attraction.

Attractor Factor

Your body language is a key component to what makes you attractive to another—or not. From your posture to your clothes to your stance to your hairstyle, as we've discussed throughout this book, all of these things express who you are and what you want. So if you want a great-looking date, be good looking yourself. If you want to get noticed, be noticeable.

WORKIN' IT

You know how it feels to be under-dressed when you walk into a nice restaurant. You're either ignored or stared at for the wrong reasons. Perform a test run by dressing up for the right kind of attention, walking into that restaurant, and seeing if that doesn't feel 100 percent better. Always dress as if you're going to meet the love of your life; you never know when they might show up.

When you pass by the same billboard seven or more times, your awareness of the advertised product increases. The same goes for repeated exposure to potential mates. The more you come face-to-face with them, the more opportunity for attraction factors to increase at each encounter.

Make the most of each encounter you may have by being prepared at all times with your body, dress, and mind-set. If you know you may encounter someone you are attracted to, position yourself accordingly. Think about in movies when a woman fluffs up her hair, puts on lipstick, stands tall, and checks her backside in the mirror before seeing a certain someone. It's the perfect example of preparing to send a message of attraction.

Eye Gazing

The most powerful connection you can have with another human being is when your eyes meet. It may seem scary to allow yourself to be vulnerable, but if you practice eye gazing techniques, your love connections will explode. Michael Ellsberg, author of *The Power of Eye Contact*, created a singles event called Eye Gazing Parties, a New York dating trend featured in *Elle* magazine.

The good news is you don't have to travel to the Big Apple to learn how to make good eye contact and experience a true felt connection with another person. Here's an eye gazing exercise to show you how it's done. Practice with a trusted friend first to get the hang of it:

- Begin by looking at your friend's right or left eye only.

- Then move your gaze to the other eye and do the same.

- When that feels comfortable, gaze into both eyes with both of yours.

- The entire exercise should take two to three minutes total.

After you've practiced on a friend, begin connecting with people you encounter in day-to-day interactions, such as servers, bank tellers, and clerks in grocery checkout lines. Make eye contact, and then maintain the gaze while making light conversation.

Make this a part of your everyday ritual, and you'll get more comfortable with eye contact and be ready when the time is right for the real romantic deal.

Don't get eye gazing confused with stalker eyes. It's not a frozen stare; it's a warm, sincere, and inviting gaze. With good eye contact, you're on your way to real authentic, face-to-face connections—something that cyber connections just can't accomplish.

Having a good eye connection leads to a better personal connection.

Historically, women are better at holding eye contact than men; but with practice, men can also master eye gazing. Men who make a higher level of eye contact are perceived as:

- More powerful
- Attentive
- Likable and more attractive
- Warm and personable

- Competent and confident
- Trustworthy, sincere, and honest
- Professionally and emotionally stable

Men who make less eye contact are perceived to be:

- Distrustful
- Suspicious
- Lacking confidence in what they're saying

- Impersonal
- Uninterested
- Inattentive

Do This

If romance has taken a back seat to other concerns lately, and you want to find a new mate or spark an old flame, here are some body language cues that will signal L-O-V-E to the person watching you.

Show Your Vulnerable Side

The neck, inside of the wrists, underarms, and ankles display a lady's vulnerable side and are an aphrodisiac for men. Visualize Richard Gere in *An Officer and a Gentleman* as he whisked away his lady-love, carrying her, neck fully exposed, arms fallen to the side, showing the inner side of her wrists and underarms. Another way you can show your vulnerable side is by tilting your neck back and gliding your hand from your earlobe down your neck to your collarbone with fingers open.

Show vulnerability with this gesture.

Guys, women are attracted to the stronger side—chiseled features; hands on hips; hands in front pockets, thumbs protruding; arms crossed; legs shoulder-width apart. Guys can show vulnerability with warmth in their eyes and a genuine, authentic smile or a concealed, suppressed smile.

Use Your Hair

When a woman is feeling sexy and attracted to someone, the hair toss to one side, exposing the neck, is a turn-on for men, but it shouldn't be overdone. Ladies with mid-length to short hair can opt for the neck glide; it works just as well.

A hair toss expresses attraction.

When a man is attracted to a woman, he signals his interest with grooming gestures. He'll look up at her while gliding his fingers through his hair, with his head slightly tilted down.

Peekaboo

Ladies, slowly slide off a barstool, allowing your skirt to rise slightly, exposing an inch or so of the outer thigh. This can be done subtly, just to catch the eye of that attractive someone sitting near you.

Also, uncrossing your legs and re-crossing them the other way can be an eye-catcher. It can trigger the memory of the moment in *Basic Instinct* with Sharon Stone that made every man's jaw drop.

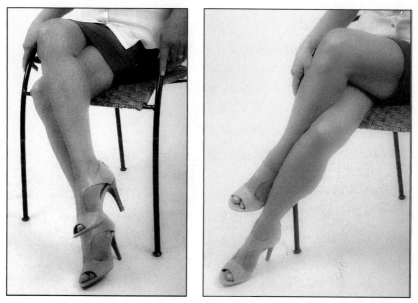

Uncrossing and recrossing legs can be a subtle seduction.

The guy equivalent of a peekaboo would be running a hand over his chest or muscles, or hands in front pockets, thumbs pointed toward their prize.

Dangle Your Shoe

Ladies can use their shoes to their advantage. Kick off the heel of your pump to dangle your shoe off the tip of your toes. Glide your hand down your leg to your ankle to push the shoe back on your heel. Keep your head and chin down while you reach down, but as your hand rises back up, glance up with just your eyes.

Stand Tall

A woman who opens her stance, taking up all the space she is occupying, shows confidence, is alluring, and is asking to be noticed. Standing with one hand on her hip, shifting her weight to one foot, hip cocked to one side, legs apart, she's saying, "Let's ride."

Men are definitely posers. You'll see them puff up their chests, stand legs shoulder width apart, suck in their bellies, and flex their biceps.

Lick Your Lips

A woman can drive a man crazy by glancing all around his face, stopping at his mouth, then licking her lips.

Glancing at his mouth, then licking her lips, is a sign she's attracted.

Men do something similar, holding eye contact and daring the woman to look away first. This is often accompanied, in bars, by a long slow drink from his beer.

Glance Over Your Shoulder

Ladies, a subtle look over your shoulder when someone attractive walks by lets him know you noticed him. Turn your head to follow him, lift your shoulder toward your chin, glance at him, and gently flutter your eyelashes.

An over-the-shoulder glance tells a guy you've taken notice.

Embrace Your Curves

What do Jennifer Lopez, Beyoncé, and Kim Kardashian have in common? Beautiful hourglass figures. Ladies, cinch in your waist with a fashionable belt and let your curves do the talking.

Show off your curves!

Remain Mysterious

Don't pick up the phone on the first ring; resist and let it go to voicemail. Appear busy, even when you're not. Don't jump on every invitation. Create a little mystique, so that anticipation builds before your date can see you. This is especially true for ladies—it definitely holds a date's interest when she's not readily available.

Don't Do This

There are as many, or even more, don'ts as there are do's when it comes to the body language of love. To mutually attract a person of interest, delete these moves from your body vocabulary altogether!

Wandering Eyes

Anyone would glance at an attractive stranger; it's human nature, like admiring fine art. But if you're on a date and your date can't control the urge to stare, chances are their eyes won't be the only thing wandering. Wandering eyes, by either side, is a no-no.

Wandering eyes show disinterest and a continued interest in exploring other options.

Back Pats

Hugging can be a good thing. But if a date hugs you and pats you on the back, this is a consoling gesture, not an intimate one. It's more appropriate when giving a baby a bottle, not making an intimate gesture or connection.

A back pat is used to console and is not a sign of attraction.

Last-Minute Invitations

No one wants to feel like an afterthought or last on the list. Don't wait until the last minute to invite that special someone on a date, or they could also think you are tardy in other areas of your life—such as paying bills, meeting deadlines, or keeping appointments.

Asking for a weekend date by mid-week shows that you respect your date's busy schedule and that you are thinking of them ahead of time.

WORKIN' IT

How you do some things in life can be taken as a reflection of how you do other things in life. Think about how your words and actions will be perceived by others.

Shifty Eyes

Eyes that dart about and don't stay focused on any one thing are hard to trust. Shifty eyes can make it more difficult to connect with someone, whether it's intentional or not.

But before you assume deception or disinterest, there could be one of several things to rule out, such as shyness, distraction, anxiousness, or attention deficit hyperactivity disorder (ADHD). Any of these can make it difficult for your date to sustain eye contact.

Shifty eyes do not allow for emotional intimacy.

Cell Phone Fascination

On Valentine's Day, at a popular sushi restaurant, you notice an attractive couple just two tables away. Instead of being present in the moment and validating his date's existence, Mr. Cool scans through the text messages on his cell phone, smiling and laughing occasionally, as he entertains himself. He doesn't notice his date's silent distress at being alone in a crowd on the most romantic night of the year.

Each time he receives or sends a text, he breaks contact with his date. Her curled-up body language signals that she is holding her frustration inside, as she looks around the restaurant out of boredom and disgust. Has he picked up the clues that he's about to be dumped on Valentine's Day? Nope! You watch as she excuses herself to visit the ladies room and never returns.

If you can't stop looking at your cell phone long enough to enjoy your date, make a date with your cell phone instead.

Put the cell phone away; she's starving for your attention, and you're showing you're really not into her.

Cold Shoulder

Turning your shoulder or even your back toward a person is saying you don't want to engage with them. The message is unmistakable. So if you like your date and want them to like you, don't give them the cold shoulder. It's not being mysterious; it's just being cold.

Don't give a date the cold shoulder treatment.

Too Much Too Soon

Ladies, keep something about you a surprise; you may catch a man's eye at first glance if you show too much skin, but you may sell yourself short with a short-lived love connection. Choose figure-fitting clothes that are tasteful and age-appropriate, and fabrics that flow gracefully around your curves, not holding them in place like a harness.

Men, don't come on too strong. Women like the dance. If you are too direct, you might chase them away.

Reading Your Date

Two or more of the following behaviors indicates that your date is losing interest or has checked out altogether:

- Glances around the room
- Looks at watch
- Angles the body away from you
- Yawns
- Stares blankly
- Leans back in chair
- Eyes unfocused
- Sighs
- Long eye closures
- Slumped body posture
- Dry glass

On the other hand, an interested date will display these behaviors:

- Maintains eye contact
- Leans forward
- Angles body toward you
- Erect or casual body posture
- Looks about your face
- Eyes sparkle
- Smiles occasionally
- Orders another round

The Least You Need to Know

- Proper eye contact is key when expressing interest in another.
- Flirtatious gestures include touching and tossing hair, dressing attractively, and glancing over your shoulder.
- Shifty eyes, turning your shoulders away, and paying more attention to your cell phone are avoidance gestures.
- Leaning forward and maintaining eye contact mean a date is interested.

References

The following articles, books, and websites were used in research for this book. Reading them in their original forms will enhance your understanding of body language.

Articles

Adam, H., and A. D. Galinsky. "Enclothed Cognition." *Journal of Experimental Social Psychology*, 2012.

Alves, A., L. De Souza, V. Baumgarten, U. Balao, and E. Otta. "Perception of Men's Personal Qualities and Prospect of Employment as a Function of Facial Hair." Department of Experimental Psychology, Institute of Psychology, University of Sao Paulo, Brazil, 2003.

Caso, L., F. Maricchiola, A. Vrij, and S. Mann. "The Impact of Deception and Suspicion on Different Hand Movements." *Journal of Nonverbal Behavior*, 30(1), 2006.

DePaulo, B. M. "Spotting Lies: Can Humans Learn to Do Better?" *Current Directions in Psychology Science*, 3, 1994: 83–86.

Ekman, P. "The Expressive Pattern of Laughter." A. W. Kaszniak, ed. 2001.

Ekman, P., and M. O'Sullivan. "The Ability to Detect Deceit Generalizes Across Different Types of High-State Lies." *Journal of Personality and Social Psychology*, 72, 1991: 1,429–1,439.

———. "Who Can Catch a Liar?" *American Psychologist*, 46, 1991: 913–920.

Ekman, P., and W. V. Freisen. "Felt, False, and Miserable Smiles." *Journal of Nonverbal Behavior*, 6(4), 1982.

———. "Smiles When Lying: Interpersonal Relations and Group Processes." *Journal of Personality and Psychology*. Volume 54, No. 3, 1988: 414–420.

———. "The Facial Action Coding System." Palo Alto, CA: Consulting Psychologists Press, 1978.

Ekman, P., M. O'Sullivan, W. V. Friesen, and Klaus Scherer, Sr. "Face, Voice, and Body Language in Detecting Deceit." *Journal of Nonverbal Behavior*, 1991.

Gillarth, O., et al. "Shoes as a Source of First Impressions." *Journal of Research in Personality*. University of Kansas, Lawrence, KS, and Wellesley College, Wellesley, MA, 2012.

Kahl, M. C. "Perceptions of Body Modifications." Department of Psychology, Loyola University, New Orleans, 2002.

Krauss, Y. C., and P. Chawla. "What Do Conversational Hand Gestures Tell Us? Nonverbal Behavior and Nonverbal Communication." Columbia University, 1991.

Lee, A., and A. Bruckman. "Judging You by the Company You Keep: Dating on Social Networking Sites." Georgia Institute of Technology, Atlanta, GA, 2007.

Matsumoto, D. "More Evidence for the Universality of a Contempt Expression." *Motivation and Emotion*. Springer, Netherlands, Volume 16, Number 4, December 1992.

McClish, M. "I Know You Are Lying: Detecting Deception Through Statement Analysis." Kearney: The Marpa Group, Inc., 2001, 2008.

Mehrabian, A. "Nonverbal Betrayal of Feeling." *Journal of Experimental Research Psychology*, 5, 1997: 64–73.

Ruch, W., and P. Ekman. "The Expressive Pattern of Laughter." Human Interaction Laboratory, University of California, 2001.

Zuckerman, M., and R. E. Driver. "Telling Lies: Verbal and Nonverbal Correlates of Deception." W. A. Seigman and S. Feldstein, eds. *Multichannel Integration of Nonverbal Behavior.* Hillsdale, NJ: Erlbaum. 1985: 129–147.

Books

Axtell, R. E. *Gestures: The Do's and Taboos of Body Language Around the World.* New York: John Wiley & Sons Inc., 1991, 1998.

Bandler, R., and J. LaValle. *Persuasion Engineering.* Capitaola, CA: Meta Publications, Inc., 1996.

Brooks, M. *Instant Rapport.* New York: Warner Business Books, 1990.

Byrne, R. *The Secret.* New York: Atria Books, 2006.

Ekman, P. *Why Kids Lie: How Parents Can Encourage Truthfulness.* New York: Penguin Books USA Inc., 2006.

———. *Telling Lies: Clues to Deceit in the Marketplace, Politics, and Marriage.* New York: W.W. Norton and Company, Ltd., 2001.

———. *Emotions Revealed: Recognizing Faces and Feelings to Improve Communication and Emotional Life.* New York: Henry Holt and Company, LLC, 2003.

Ekman, P., and W. V. Freisen. *Unmasking the Face: A Guide to Recognizing Emotions from Facial Expressions.* Cambridge, MA: Malor Books, 2003.

Ellsberg, M. *The Power of Eye Contact: Your Secret for Success in Business, Love, and Life.* New York: Harper, 2010.

Hogan, K. *The Psychology of Persuasion: How to Persuade Others to Your Way of Thinking.* Gretna, LA: Pelican Publishing Company, 2005.

Hwang, S. H., D. Matsumoto, and G. Frank. *Nonverbal Communication Science and Applications.* Thousand Oaks, CA: Sage Publications, Inc., 2013.

Mack, A., and I. Rock. *Inattentional Blindness.* Cambridge, MA: MIT Press, 1998.

Pennebaker, J. A. *The Secret Life of Pronouns: What Your Words Say About You.* New York: Bloomsbury Press, 2011.

Stacks, D., M. Hickson, and N. Moore. *Nonverbal Communication: Studies and Applications, 5th Ed.* USA: Oxford University Press, 2009.

Websites

Color Psychology:

precisionintermedia.com/color.html

empower-yourself-with-color-psychology.com/meaning-of-colors.html

Detecting Lies:

smithsonianmag.com/science-nature/lie.html?c=y&story=fullstory

Identifying Liars:

news.bbc.co.uk/go/pr/fr/-/2/hi/health/3743448.stm

Lie to Me:

popularmechanics.com/science/4300722

Picking Election Winners by Appearance 70 Percent of the Time:

science20.com

Smart Coat:

everydayhealth.com/emotional-health/0405/could-wearing-a-lab-coat-make-you-smarter.aspx

Answers

In certain chapters in this book, you've been challenged to demonstrate what you've learned. Here are the answers.

Chapter 1

Find the clues:

The photo of delivery trucks on the bookshelves suggests that the man works for some kind of delivery company. Other clues suggest it is a nonprofit accepting gently used furniture and clothing.

The ceramic hand on the desk could be a tchotchke, or it may have something to do with the organization's mission, which seems to be lending a helping hand to others in need.

The awards in the background suggest that he is good at what he does.

The man practices "organized disorganization." He has some semblance of order—piles. He has his own form of organization that works for him.

His personality is likable and friendly per his very natural expression. He fits the environment he is in.

From his starched shirt and tie, you can surmise that he holds a position of authority.

What else did you gather?

Chapter 2

1. What is the appropriate amount of eye contact in a face-to-face encounter?

   B. 70–80 percent (More than that is perceived as awkward staring; less comes across as inattentive.)

2. When making eye contact with your customer, where do you focus your eyes?

   A. From the tip of the nose to the outer corners of the eyes (We connect through eye contact. The mouth and below is distracting. You break eye contact.)

3. Which best describes your handshaking style?

   D. None of the above (A firm web-to-web handshake with two to three pumps while making eye contact is generally considered the most appropriate and effective handshake in any endeavor.)

4. How do you prefer to make a sales pitch?

   C. Build rapport and trust first; then ask the customer to tell me about his or her business (People do business with people they like and trust. Rapport building is key.)

5. When listening to a customer's complaint, I …

   B. Lean slightly forward; tilt my head occasionally; and nod, signaling I understand (Active listening shows interest and engagement. The customer should feel that you are present and focused on him and his concern.)

6. What color do you wear to build trust?

   B. Blue (Studies have shown that wearing blue evokes trust and loyalty.)

7. Which best describes the way you would present a proposal to a customer face-to-face?

   C. Place the proposal in the center of the table, and let the customer reach for it (No one likes to be handed anything. Placing the proposal in the center of the table allows the customer to take ownership.)

8. If you are a man, when meeting a prospect, what would you wear?

   B. Dress pants, sport coat, buttoned shirt, and tie (You don't want to come in as the "power guy"; you want to establish rapport.)

   If you are a woman, what would you wear to meet a male business prospect?

   D. Any of the above (Avoid wearing anything provocative. Dress age and circumstance appropriate.)

9. During a sales call, what do you usually think about?

   B. Finding solutions to meet the customer's needs (If you don't know a customer's needs, you can't find solutions.)

10. If you could ask your prospects what they thought of you, what do you think they'd say?

    C. Confident and competent (In business, people want to know that you will get the job done well.)

Chapter 4

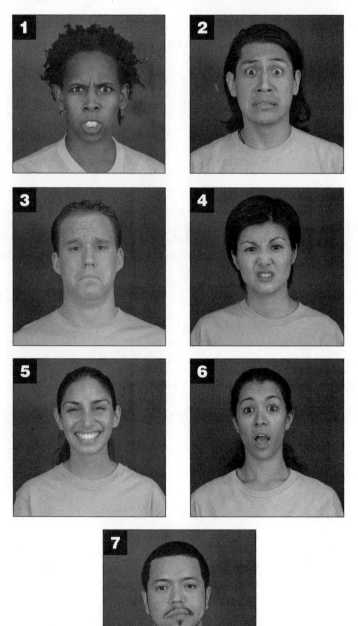

1. Anger—Frustration to rage: Man with squinted eyes, lowered eyebrows, and jutting jaw, gritting his teeth

2. Fear—Physical or mental harm: Man with wide eyes, raised eyebrows, flared nostrils, and frowning mouth

3. Sadness—Suffering, loss, disappointment, hopelessness, or grief: Man with furrowed forehead, raised eyebrows, and frowning mouth

4. Disgust—Repulsion, aversions from mild to intense: Woman with furrowed forehead, raised eyebrows, wrinkled nose, and gritted teeth

5. Happiness—Contentment to extreme joy and fulfillment: Woman with wide smile and squinted eyes

6. Surprise—Briefest, fleeting emotion from an unexpected event: Lady with eyes and mouth forming circles and raised eyebrows

7. Contempt—Feelings of superiority over others: Man with hard stare and mouth twisted to the side

Chapter 17

Note that most people exhibit multiple, or "cluster" responses. For example, a critical person might also be skeptical, resistant, and suspicious.

From left to right:

1. Hands under table, looking down: Disengaged

2. Hands under table, not looking at speaker: Disengaged

3. Speaker—hands facing, basketball-gripping gesture, asking for cooperation: Engaged

4. Left eyebrow raised, hand on forehead: Skeptical

5. Cup in front (barrier), breaking eye contact: Guarded

6. Leaning head to side: Engaged

7. Leaning forward, looking at speaker: Engaged

8. Manipulating hands, mouth appears strained: Anxious

9. Closed fist, mouth clenched, furrowed eyebrows, hand on hip: Angry

10. Eyes wide open, mouth stretched in contempt, hands on hip: Suspicious, skeptical

11. Hand on table, pointed toward speaker, open and receptive: Engaged

Index